Having completed his training as a paediatric surgeon in France, **Professor Elahi** had a distinguished ᵤemic career and a successful clinical practice. As ᵤean of three schools of medicine in Iran, he has published numerous textbooks, several of which are authoritative treatises on anatomy that are used as reference books today. In addition to his professional endeavours, Professor Elahi has extensively researched the topic of spirituality. Inspired by the innovative and universal philosophy of his father, he has written several books on the subject, notably *La Voie de la Perfection* (Albin Michel, 1992, 4th ed.) – a systematic synthesis of the eternal spiritual and esoteric laws that transcends religions, cultures and human conventions. Since its publication in 1976, *La Voie* has been translated into seven languages (*The Path of Perfection*, Element Books, 1993).

by the same author

The Way of Light
The Path of Perfection

Foundations of Natural Spirituality

A SCIENTIFIC APPROACH TO THE NATURE OF THE SPIRITUAL SELF

BAHRAM ELAHI

ELEMENT

Shaftesbury, Dorset ● Rockport, Massachusetts
Melbourne, Victoria

© Element Books 1997
Text and illustrations © Bahram Elahi 1997
Translation by Richard Ross and Edward Davis

First published in France, 1996, by Éditions Dervy as
Fondemements de la spiritualité naturelle

This edition first published in Great Britain in 1997 by
Element Books Limited
Shaftesbury, Dorset SP7 8BP

Published in the USA in 1997 by
Element Books, Inc.
PO Box 830, Rockport, MA 01966

Pubished in Australia in 1997 by
Element Books
and distributed by Penguin Australia Limited
487 Maroondah Highway, Ringwood, Victoria 3134

Cover design by Slatter-Anderson
Page design by Roger Lightfoot
Typeset by Footnote Graphics, Warminster, Wilts
Printed and bound in the U.K. by
J W Arrowsmith Ltd, Bristol

British Library Cataloguing in Publication
data available

Library of Congress Cataloging in Publication Data
Elahi, Bahram
    Foundations of natural spirituality : our deep
need for soul and spirit / Bahram Elahi.
        p.   cm.
    Includes bibliography and index.
    ISBN 1-86204-238-1 (pbk.)
    1. Spirituality.   2. Spiritual life.   I. Title.
BL624.E44   1998   97-39504
291.4—dc21   CIP

ISBN 1 86204 238 1

Contents

When a human being reflects on his origin, his destination and the reason why he is in this world, he has arrived at the stage of self-knowledge. The essential condition for attaining self-knowledge is to become a true human being – that is, to want for others what one desires for oneself. The practice of this maxim enables a human being to reach a point where all the qualities inherent in humanity naturally emanate from him.

Ostad Elahi

List of Figures

Note to the Reader

- Ostad Elahi says: 'On the path of Truth, there is no distinction between religions, races, men and women.' Therefore, wherever masculine words or pronouns are used throughout the text, they should naturally be understood in their neutral sense.

- Most of the quotations from in this work are from a two-volume collection of Ostad Elahi's oral teachings, *Asar ol-haqq* (Traces of the Truth), which will be abridged as 'AH 1' for volume 1 and 'AH 2' for volume 2.

- All references to Bahram Elahi's *The Path of Perfection* will be abridged as 'PP'.

- Although each study in this book is an independent and complete examination of a particular subject, overall comprehension is best achieved by following the given sequence of chapters.

Editor's Preface

A graduate of the University of Montpellier Medical School in France, Bahram Elahi led a successful clinical practice alongside a distinguished academic career as professor of anatomy and paediatric surgery. During his tenure as dean of three schools of medicine in Iran he published numerous medical textbooks, several of which are authoritative treatises on anatomy. Parallel to his professional career, he has conducted extensive research in the field of spirituality. Inspired by the innovative and universal philosophy of his father, Ostad Elahi, he has written a number of books on the subject in Persian and French, notably *La Voie de la Perfection* (Albin Michel, 1992, 4th ed.), which has been translated into seven languages (*The Path of Perfection*, Element Books, 1993). Since his retirement, Professor Elahi has devoted all his time to framing a consistent and exhaustive system of spiritual thought based on Ostad Elahi's philosophy, writing books and lecturing at academic institutions throughout Europe and North America.

His most recent book, intended both for new readers and those already acquainted with Ostad Elahi's philosophy, is a compilation of lectures originally presented at the Sorbonne in Paris. *Foundations of Natural Spirituality* is not merely a general introduction to spiritual thinking or simply another philosophy of life; rather, as the title suggests, it provides a complete reformation of what we have been accustomed to understand by the concept of spirituality. Indeed, Ostad Elahi often emphasized the necessity of redefining spiritual theory and practice in a way that would not only fit the spirit of modern times, but which would also bring out its true essence while still preserving the core of all religions. This work essentially provides the philosophical ground plan for this reexamination of the basics of spirituality, setting forth some of its more concrete and practical implications in the process.

Consequently, in comparison to *The Path of Perfection*, *Foundations* appears not so much a complete system as it does a preliminary exploration of a range of problems: an engaging journey through a continent of concepts, analysing experiences which, although familiar to most of us, remain difficult to express in a clear and rational manner. The challenge of this book, then, is to lay the indispensable foundation for any coherent approach to spiritual matters. This aim is achieved through extensive recourse to the apparatus of modern science and the method of analogy. Traditional concepts such as the soul, the body, consciousness and faith are therefore redefined in terms of an organic process of growth.

A reading of *Foundations* also makes it clear that such a perspective is bound to transcend all cultural, racial and religious barriers. In fact, in the author's mind, the very idea of a foundation points to a dimension of universality which prevails within all traditions. Non-confessional yet religious and spiritual, the 'foundational' approach provides a basis for the kind of mutual respect that is so essential for fruitful inter-faith dialogue.

But why speak of a *natural* spirituality? This is where the author's views are likely to seem most challenging. One of the goals of these lectures, of course, is to elaborate on this proposition and to reach a proper understanding of all its implications. Naturally, the kind of explanation that a brief preface provides cannot replace a thorough reading.

However, the title itself is sufficiently puzzling to demand a certain amount of clarification. To speak of 'natural spirituality' requires, first and foremost, that the spiritual realm be viewed as no less natural than the realm of physical nature. The consequences of this assumption are easy to deduce: spiritual processes abide by precise laws, as do all other natural processes, and there are consistent conditions, requirements and structures which, in terms of one's spiritual destiny, cannot be avoided. The claim is at once pragmatic and scientific: 'anything goes' is an adage that does not hold in spirituality, at least no more than it does in any other scientific discipline.

Another aspect of this natural quality of spirituality consists in its adaptation to the spirit of human beings. This is where the universal aspect of this reflection once again resurfaces. If the traditional movements of religion and spirituality have lost touch with the masses and have come to be regarded as incompatible or even alien to the pre-occupations of people in modern societies, it may well be because these movements have been unable to express the natural and rational heart of their message. In other words, they have fallen short in presenting a straightforward and coherent depiction of spiritual matters that is suitable to the level of intelligence and understanding of today's society. Not surprisingly, then, one of the most forceful assertions contained in these studies is that spirituality, far from being a patchwork of obscure and esoteric teachings, is in fact a coherent discipline that anyone can engage in, provided that one is equipped with the proper tools and an adequate understanding of the principles.

Introduction

The reason for this introduction is that the reader is entitled to know a little more about who is talking in this book and what his motivations are.

I am a professor of anatomy and paediatric surgery, which I have practised and taught for some 30 years. I do not mention my title or my professional accomplishments to confer authority on my words but rather to emphasize that I am familiar with rational thinking and the scientific approach. I have always tackled problems, including questions of man's metaphysical destiny, with a scientific mind, in other words, in a rational, pragmatic and concrete manner, trying to remain true to myself, my Creator and my fellow human beings. By stating my profession, I also wish to make it clear that spirituality is not my trade – that is, I do not gain any personal profit from spirituality. Jesus once said: 'You have been given freely; give freely.' That is what all authentic spiritual personalities have done, and we, too, should do the same.

Although born and raised in a family with deep mystical roots, I was not always attracted to spirituality. Until the age of 33, I was completely oblivious of man's spiritual dimension, and my reasoning was based solely on my mental self, which I considered my total self. At that time – which corresponded with the end of my studies – I met someone who triggered a process within me similar to the transition that occurs from childhood to adolescence, only this process took place on a spiritual level. In the same way that a specific biological process transforms the mental awareness of a child and awakens him to new feelings and instincts, a similar process governs the natural and progressive growth of the soul, through which our soul develops and our attitude towards spirituality evolves. This meeting awakened in me the love of God and uncovered the deep and real awareness I had been unconscious of, as if I had recovered from a long amnesia. This profound awareness makes us realize that physical death is not the end of our existence, and that our material life is nothing but a preliminary, albeit necessary, stage of our real life, which is eternal.

Since this awakening, my only concern has been to attend assiduously to both the spiritual and material dimensions of life, for as long as we live in this physical world, the two dimensions are intertwined and interact continuously. So, for more than 30 years I have been studying, practising and assimilating a spirituality which I call 'natural' under the careful supervision of an exceptional being, about whom I unfortunately cannot say all that I know, for this individual was my father and anything I say would be attributed to filial love. I will therefore leave the discovery of this man's genius to others. However, according to the opinions of those who know him – some simply through the recent exhibition on his life and works[1] – Ostad Elahi was an extraordinary person and a humanist in the true sense of the word.

Ostad Elahi was a philosopher, and a judge by profession and a musician. During the first third of his life he lived in complete seclusion from the world like the traditional mystics, leading a life devoted to ascetic practice and contemplation. In his later years he would say that these were the happiest days of his life. Yet, to build upon and to improve his mystical experience, he embraced a judicial career at the age of 36, thus putting his ethical principles to the test in the crucible of society. It is hard to appreciate fully the difficulty of exchanging an angelic, mystical lifestyle for one in the midst of society, to say nothing of the sensitive professional commitment that accompanied this radical change.

From then on and until the end of his life, Ostad Elahi practised spirituality in the heart of society. A prominent journalist once noted: 'The traditional mystics withdrew from society to lead a life of ascetic contemplation, whereas Ostad Elahi took the opposite path, thereby accomplishing the seemingly impossible.' In traditional mysticism, material life and spiritual life were incompatible; Ostad Elahi made them compatible by adapting the practice of spirituality to life in society. In fact, Ostad Elahi devoted his entire life to elucidating the true origin and nature of human beings, their rights and duties, and their final destination. His research and experiments have resulted in a rational, coherent and practical system of thought known as 'natural spirituality' – a spirituality adapted to the people of our times which he described as a medicine of the soul.[2] What I am presenting to you in this series of studies is the result of Ostad Elahi's own research, to the extent that I have practised and assimilated it.

Ostad Elahi used to say: 'As long as I have not put something into practice, I will not prescribe it to others; everything that I say has first been examined in depth.' Consequently, throughout these lectures one should not expect to hear purely intellectual speculations on problems of the soul or the destiny of man. By nature, I am only interested in the kind of knowledge that has practical and concrete implications. I am one of those people who always think in terms of: 'What is the use of this?' 'On what elements is it based?' 'Do these elements correspond to real truths?' For quite a long time now, it is with this frame of mind that I have sought to assimilate certain 'real truths',

truths which will enable me to know and accomplish my essential duties so that I may benefit progressively from the rights granted to us human beings by the Creator.

Why am I presenting this work at all? First, because it is my duty as a human being to convey the results of my research when it may benefit others; to keep it to myself would be a breach of duty towards my fellow beings. Second, to establish that spirituality is a science, despite what people commonly think. When compared to the various kinds of so-called 'rational' discourse, the prevalent view nowadays is that spirituality is merely a matter of intuition, personal feeling and subjective belief, which would seem to imply that it is beyond the grasp of reason and thus incapable of objective assessment.

Well, I am convinced of the opposite. Spiritual truths are far more precise than the inflexible laws that we traditionally associate with the physical universe. If the word 'science' has a meaning, it should apply to spirituality as well, perhaps even more so than to all the disciplines which we naturally consider to be scientific. Indeed, spiritual phenomena, processes and stages of development abide by extremely rigorous laws and rules, and it is the function of a spiritual system to establish and elucidate these rules. The following studies, I hope, will make it clear that spirituality is not a domain that can be left to the fantasy of esoteric inspiration or to amateur improvisation. Rather, it is a serious field of research which requires a scientific frame of mind, along with a constant concern for the most appropriate description, image and formulation.

Of course, each science has its own logic, its own mode of reasoning and experimentation, and its own way of establishing what is objective. When we shift from the study of biological systems to the study of human societies, we have to adapt to a new set of concepts and to new forms of reasoning and measurement. In the same way, when we shift from the physical dimension to the spiritual one, we are confronted with a new form of logic. Actually, the spiritual dimension encompasses physical reality and can account for it, whereas the reverse is not yet true. Not only does spiritual objectivity not contradict physical objectivity, but if spiritual truths cannot be weighed with today's physical tools, that is because the experimental sciences are still insufficiently advanced to do so.

This brings us to a common objection directed against spirituality being a science – namely, the apparent lack of measuring tools in the field of spirituality. The answer to this can be derived from what we have just said: objectivity and instrumentation should be adapted to each science. The instruments used in physical sciences today are meant to convey information through the physical senses, whereas the instruments of spiritual sciences are suited to the spiritual senses. Yes, there are spiritual instruments, but they make sense only to those who have developed their spiritual senses. Spiritual objectivity is a tangible fact only for those who have awakened and educated their spiritual senses, just as a false note in a symphony is perceived only by the conductor and a few listeners. Anyone can develop competence in, say, biology, provided he goes through the long process of training and study which leads to such competence. In the same way, anyone can attain spiritual knowledge, provided that he develops the proper faculties through proper education. Regarding the education of the human soul, Ostad Elahi says: 'The soul's process of perfection may be compared to academic studies: it must complete its classes, one by one, after assimilating them.'

I would like to add that the spiritual world is the world of the obvious: its truths must ultimately be ascertained through direct observation – which does not mean that these truths should not be presented as methodically and rigorously as possible. In any discipline, one can always reject the foundations of a system for being arbitrary, despite the fact that no reasonable grounds exist for doing so. In this respect, spirituality is no different from other sciences, and my approach cannot overcome this kind of objection. The truth of a theory, however, must be judged by its coherence, and above all, the results it yields. One may reject the axioms of geometry on the grounds that they have not been proven, but then building even a small bridge will become an extremely difficult task. For those who have not yet developed the aptitude to see the truth, one cannot convey anything through pure mental reasoning; one can only tell such people to take the same road the great spiritual saints have taken if they, too, wish to see and experience what those saints did.

At any rate, even if one is not prepared to consider spirituality as a science in its own right, one should agree at least that it is more fruitful – and less dangerous – to approach spirituality with a rational mind, if only to distinguish between useful knowledge and spiritual amusements so as to avoid falling into unscrupulous hands. When confronted with a spiritual path, it is always better to consider everything in a rational way and to bear in mind a few basic criteria. For instance, if an allegedly spiritual person derives some personal profit from spirituality, one should reasonably infer that this individual is not a true spiritual person. How can we consider someone who compromises his dignity by living off others as a spiritual model? Intellectual abilities should also be taken into account: would it be reasonable to expect guidance from a simple-minded person? In fact, I think the best examples are the great saints and prophets, and we should base our criteria on them. They were all normal, intelligent people who led normal lives. They were spiritual geniuses, yet this did not induce any extravagant behaviour on their part.

The current state of spirituality in the world is comparable to that of the sciences before the rise of modern physics. In the obscure landscape of today's spirituality, where many religious and mystical trends mix with pseudo-religions and cults, it is essential that we make good use of our powers of reasoning to discriminate between true and false. The main purpose of this work is to draw the attention of my contemporaries to the fact that spirituality is not a game. It deals with nothing less than reality. Therefore, it must not be taken lightly or left to the whims of our fantasies. There is a faculty in human beings which enables them, whenever they collectively make an effort and focus their attention on a problem, to make authentic discoveries and to arrive at real truths. I am quite confident that once people become aware that spirituality is an experimental science, which must be approached with a scientific mind, the spiritual outlook of today's world will undergo a radical change.

Bahram Elahi

[1] The centennial of Ostad Elahi's birth was celebrated in September 1995 in different countries (Paris: La Sorbonne; London: University of London; New York: New York University School of Law; Los Angeles: University of California Los Angeles) under the patronage, in France, of Unesco, the Ministry of Culture, the Paris Education Offices and others. In Paris, an exhibition was also devoted to the life and works of Ostad Elahi (Chapelle de la Sorbonne, September–October 1995).

[2] For more information on the distinction between natural spirituality and other forms of spirituality, see the lecture presented by the author in the Acta of the symposium: 'Spirituality: Plurality and Unity', Presses de l'Universite de Paris–Sorbonne (pp. 128–133).

Preliminary Study

The Rights and Duties of Human Beings

Rights. The Primordial Right; Necessary Rights: Universal Innate Rights and Potential Rights. **Duties.** Determined Duties; Free Duties. **Duties of Human Beings.** Duties towards Oneself; Duties towards God; Duties towards Others. **Conclusion.**

In the course of this first lecture, we will see that the existence and purpose of all beings can be summarized in two words: rights and duties. This statement may seem somewhat reductive, but we will examine it in its entirety by considering the various rights and duties of creatures, as well as the role of these two words in the destiny of every being.

Rights

Every being has two kinds of rights: primordial rights and necessary rights.

Every being that comes into existence is naturally endowed with a *primordial right*: the right to reach the goal for which it has been created. In other words, the right to fully benefit, in proportion to its capacity, from the divine grace. In order to achieve this primordial right, every being has access to a number of means called **necessary rights**; these rights refer to all the means or tools the Creator has granted His creatures so that they may benefit from their primordial right.

Among these necessary rights, some are granted from the outset to all creatures, whereas others are acquired through one's own efforts. The former are known as **universal innate rights** and the latter as **potential rights**.

The universal innate rights are as follows:

- The feeling or state of existence. This feeling or sensation of oneself can be found at all levels of creation,[1] from minerals (and even lower levels) to humans. Generally, this feeling manifests itself through a sense of well-being.

- The instinct of preservation (the faculty of struggling to stay alive).

- The faculty of 'attracting benefit' and 'rejecting loss', meaning the faculty of choosing what is useful and beneficial, and rejecting or avoiding what is harmful or injurious. Take cats, for example. They are carnivorous animals, yet sometimes they instinctively set out to eat special herbs that have a healing effect on them. This seemingly unnatural behaviour is a result of that very faculty of 'attracting benefit'.

Apart from these universal innate rights, there are also potential rights. To achieve potential rights, all creatures must first carry out the duties they have been assigned. For example, every being has the potential right of feeding himself, but to do so he must observe certain duties. One of the potential rights of humans is to become the highest being among creation; for this to occur, however, many duties must first be carried out.

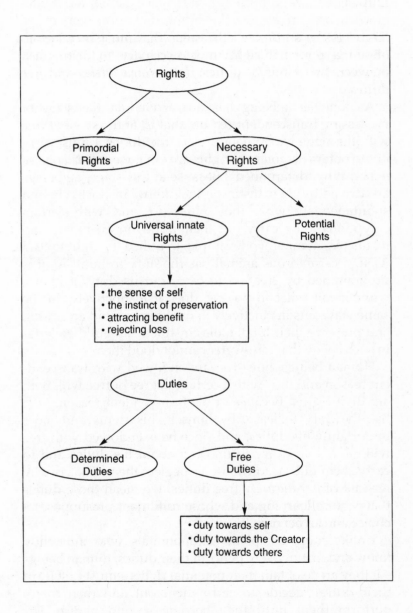

Duties

'Duty' is the sum of all the steps that must be taken to obtain a potential right. It is necessary to distinguish between two kinds of duties: *determined duties* and *free duties*.

As long as a being has not arrived at the stage of possessing transcendent reason, that is, at the stage of free will (the stage we humans are at), the duties it must carry out to obtain its potential rights are what we call *determined duties*. Why 'determined'? Because at this stage, all beings are driven by their instincts; they know instinctively and spontaneously what they must do, and with certain exceptions, they carry out their duties in an innate and instinctive manner. For example, to utilize the right to feed itself, a carnivorous animal has the duty to hunt. As it is programmed by creation to carry out its duty, it knows without fail what to do and does it instinctively. In the same way, ants instinctively know how to build an ant-hill and preserve their food; moles instinctively build galleries in such a way that rain-water cannot flood them.

Human beings, however, are endowed with transcendent reason and thus with a certain degree of free will. Both are divine gifts. Because of his transcendent reason, man has the duty to learn, by himself, his rights and more importantly his duties, and since he is endowed with free will, he is free to try to find out about his duties and to carry them out, or to choose to neglect them. That is why we talk of *free duty*. By free duties, we mean those duties that require learning and whose fulfilment presupposes a choice and an act of will.

Unlike minerals, plants and animals who inherently know and instinctively perform their duties, human beings – if they are to obtain their potential rights – must first learn their duties, decide to carry them out and then try to perform them until they become second nature. For example, to actualize the right to be respected, human beings have the duty to respect the rights of others and to develop this quality within themselves to the extent that it becomes a second nature. Or, if a person does not wish to be marginalized by society, he has a duty to conform to certain social rules. Similarly, in spirituality, if an individual wishes to obtain his right to draw closer to God, he has an obligation to accomplish his duties as a spiritual student in this school we call Earth.

The Duties of Human Beings

Our first duty as human beings is to seek to know who and what we really are. We will then discover that we are bi-dimensional beings, meaning that, in addition to our visible physical dimension, we also have a metaphysical dimension that is not apparent to our ordinary senses. From this, we can deduce that we have two kinds of duties: those which concern our physical dimension, and those which concern our metaphysical dimension. Knowledge of our duties is not an innate part of our nature, so we have the responsibility to develop this body of knowledge and with the frame of mind of a serious student, try to find out what our duties consist of.

Religious, social, political and scientific institutions have assumed the responsibility of defining the duties that relate to our physical and temporal dimension; to know these duties, it suffices to refer to such institutions. The focus here will be on the duties which concern our metaphysical self or our real eternal self. We should point out, however, that there is no absolute dividing line between the rights and duties specific to our physical dimension and those concerning our metaphysical dimension. In fact, they all have a common divine origin because there is only one Creator. Therefore, the duties which concern our physical self are necessarily included in the duties related to our metaphysical self.

In order to learn our metaphysical duties, we must refer to authentic divine messengers, who have the mission, among other things, to reveal the duties that the Creator has assigned to human beings. The best line of conduct is to follow these duties of divine origin, for who knows better than He what is best suited to our metaphysical nature and what is good or bad for us? Thus, the Creator does not impose duties in an arbitrary way; in fact, He lets us know what we must do if we wish to develop our true nature and eventually to reach our goal of perfection.

By referring to what the divine messengers have told us, it is possible to distinguish between various kinds of metaphysical duties:

a) Duties towards ourselves, which can be further divided into two categories:

• Duties towards our body. The body has a right to be fed, clothed, kept in good health, taken care of and treated when ill, entertained within the limits of what is licit etc. For example, we have a duty to avoid anything that causes physical or psychological harm, such as alcohol and drugs, as well as anything that entails addiction and is detrimental to the integrity of our reason and will.

• Duties towards our soul. In order to maintain its health and to allow for its natural growth, our soul has the right to have access to true principles and a spiritual practice suited to its nature.

b) Duties towards our Creator:

Among these duties, the most important is to have our attention focused upon Him. Why turn our attention towards the Creator? Does He need our attention? In fact, we are the real beneficiaries of this duty towards the

Creator, because attention to the Divine is as essential for the natural development of our soul as sunlight is for the natural growth of a plant. The plant needs the sun, whereas the sun does not in any way need the plant. Similarly, if we have a duty to turn our attention towards God, it is only to benefit from His light; He has no need of our attention. Moreover, although the plant does not have the possibility of moving towards the sun, whereas we have the choice and the possibility of directing our soul towards the Divine rays. Other duties towards God are reliances, gratitude etc.

c) Duties towards others:

This category primarily involves our duties towards family, friends, our fellow beings, society at large etc. Although our duties towards others are numerous, they can be reduced to one golden rule: to act towards others as we would like others to act towards us, bearing in mind that we should respect our duties towards ourselves. Often we infringe upon the rights of others without necessarily realizing it; common examples include disturbing our neighbour's tranquillity, backbiting, mocking others, breaking our promises, breaking others' hearts, trying to rob a colleague of an opportunity or mistreating an animal. Respecting the rights of others is an essential duty, for if God is ready in His clemency to forgive the neglect or non-observance of His own right, He will never forgive a violation of another being's right, because His justice requires that He be answerable for the rights of all creatures, especially victims. Consequently, He does not allow Himself to forgive that which concerns the rights of others, instead leaving the pardon in the hands of the one who has been wronged.

Conclusion

To understand how important adequate knowledge of our rights and duties is for our spiritual development, we may compare the requirements for spiritual maturation to the preparation and technology required for launching a satellite into orbit. The 'spatial launcher' or rocket is designed to help the satellite reach its orbit. This rocket is made up of several stages, each of which provides part of the required momentum. First, the rocket is propelled by the lower stage; when the fuel tank for that stage is empty, it drops off and the next stage takes over. In this way, the rocket is able to accelerate and overcome the force of gravity. At the end of the flight, the last stage falls away and the only thing remaining is the satellite itself, which scientists refer to as the 'service and command module'.

By analogy, we could say that our current body is but one of the many stages of the multistage rocket that gradually drop off during its journey. To reach one's goal is thus to shed these series of bodies and to be launched into orbit; in this way, our metaphysical self – or the 'service and command module' – is brought into proximity with the Divine after completing its trajectory of perfection.

For a satellite to be launched into orbit, certain precise conditions must be met at every level of conception and realization. To simplify things to an extreme, we can distinguish between two fundamental elements:

- Guidance: in the case of a multistage rocket, this element is entrusted to scientists such as physicists, engineers and pilots. But for the perfection of the soul, we ourselves are in charge of the trajectory as long as we are here on earth.

- Fuel: a special quality fuel allows for lift-off of the multistage rocket and helps it to maintain its force of propulsion. Likewise, a special-quality fuel is needed to perfect the soul. This fuel essentially consists of our actions and intentions, and its quality depends on the degree to which our actions and intentions correspond with the duties we must carry out to benefit from our rights. The same act, when performed with a different degree of faith and a different intention, will produce a different kind of fuel; depending on its quality, it will produce coal, crude oil, wood, etc. To produce a fuel which is suited to our soul, we need to know in what we must have faith, whom to believe in, how to conduct ourselves and what our goal is.

Human beings must accomplish this entire process by themselves, although they do have at their disposal the help of instructors or guides. These instructors are the prophets and authentic saints, all the divine messengers whose role is to educate mankind, whether directly or indirectly, and to supervise their actions. But if we want to benefit from their guidance, we have the duty to turn towards them, to search for the right formulas revealed by God through the intermediary of His messengers, and to try to understand and to eventually apply these formulas.

If we carry out our duties correctly, we will obtain from our Creator the right to have Him accompany us on this path and guide us Himself through intuition and inspiration, or through the agency of another person who has already covered some distance and is a few steps ahead of us on the path. If we follow this forerunner, we too will forge ahead and acquire the right to have our fellow humans benefit from what we have learned.

Questions

You have said that spirituality should not be a means for making personal profit. But in the past, artists such as Michelangelo created spiritual masterpieces from which they made a living.

These artists did not sell spirituality; they just sold their art.

Why shouldn't spirituality be a source of material profit?

Pure spirituality and material profit are incompatible because spirituality is neutralized as soon as any material profit is derived from it. If someone came along pretending to be Christ and asked for a single dime for his guidance, I would immediately know he was not the one he claimed to be. By the way, if young people today understood this basic principle, they would be protected against most of the trickeries under a religious or spiritual guise which, unfortunately, are currently on the rise.

Among the universal innate rights, there is the right to experience the feeling or sensation of existence, which as you mentioned earlier, manifests itself through a sense of well-being. Well, many people do not feel or sense that well-being.

I said that, generally speaking, the feeling of existence manifests itself through a sense of well-being. This is true of all creatures. As far as human beings are concerned, however, because they are responsible beings other factors such as spiritual accountability and reactions to actions come into play – all of which are likely to alter that sensation. In general, everyone prefers the state of being or existence to nothingness. In hospitals you find people who are suffering terribly and who expect nothing more from life, and yet they are not ready to give up their existence.

You have said that the duties concerning our physical dimension are addressed by institutions, religious institutions in particular. But in my view, religious institutions are more concerned with our metaphysical dimension.

The primary duty of religious institutions is to educate the metaphysical dimension of human beings. As a result of certain circumstances that have to do with time and place, however, they have been compelled to intervene more and more in the social life of their followers, at the expense of their primary duty, which has consequently been neglected.

How can we learn the hierarchy and priorities of our duties?

Knowing the hierarchy and priorities of our duties requires a substantial amount of training. In the beginning one makes errors, but gradually, with the benefit of experience, our knowledge increases and we learn to better understand what needs to be done.

You said that we must respect our own rights and the rights of others. But how is it possible to sacrifice one's own right for the benefit of someone else's right?

To give up one's own right in favour of somebody else's right is a good thing to do, but only under certain conditions. First, this renunciation must not bring about an irreparable loss. Second, this renunciation must only concern yourself; in other words, it must not infringe on another person's right nor on that of society as a whole. Lastly, the person in favour of whom you are relinquishing your right must deserve it.

You said that the existence and purpose of all beings can be summarized in two words: rights and duties. But isn't this somewhat restrictive? How is it possible to reduce love, for example, to rights and duties?

Love is an integral part of the universal innate right called 'attracting benefit'.

You have said that all creatures possess the universal innate right to distinguish between that which is beneficial and that which is harmful to them, but there are many people who do not make that distinction and who consequently act against their own interests by making wrong choices.

In the case of human beings, the universal innate rights only concern their physical dimension and not their metaphysical one because the angelic soul in human beings, unlike other creatures, carries the Divine particle. As a result, human beings enjoy a special status.

If we carry out our duties, we will obtain the right to have our Creator accompany us. Does this mean that God Himself has duties, such as that of accompanying us, as long as we fulfil the requirements?

God has made it incumbent upon Himself to guide every person who sincerely wants to be guided and who carries out his duties. God has also made it incumbent upon Himself to place the principles and duties which are necessary for the development of the soul at the disposal of every person who sincerely seeks the truth. Search and you shall find. If you do not find, then take the principles which are common to all revealed religions and put them into practice; that is sufficient. If you put them into practice on your own, then whatever your religion, God shall guide you. He is with everyone at all times.

How can we tell whether the voice which speaks inside us and prescribes our duties comes from God or not?

If someone who has never studied medicine asks me how to diagnose a certain illness, I can never respond adequately because that person lacks the necessary knowledge to understand my answer. I would tell that individual to first go and learn the basics of medicine. Well, your question is somehow of the same kind. Generally speaking, one could say that any 'voice' or intuition suggesting that you do something which even indirectly entails an illicit material pleasure should be ignored. On the other hand, if this 'voice' suggests something that is in accord with the authentic principles of religion, law, ethics and morality, then it should be considered as true.

'Any voice or intuition suggesting that you do something which even indirectly entails an illicit material pleasure should be ignored.' But you also stated that one of our duties is to entertain our body. To entertain, it would seem, implies physical pleasure.

To look for physical pleasure in the material realm is a legitimate thing to do; it is seeking pleasure under the guise of spirituality that is reproachable.

If I have understood properly, we must carry out all our duties as human beings to acquire the aptitude to rejoin God. But how can this be sufficient motivation when we do not know who and what God is?

The only thing I can tell you is that God is so – I was going to say marvellous – but there is truly no word which can describe God. When you really experience Him, even for a millionth of a second, you will never be able to do without Him again. Nothing, no sensation, even the most extraordinary, can equal that millionth of a second during which you truly experience God. All the mystics, all the saints who have sacrificed their lives, have done so for the love of God, to draw nearer to Him and to feel the Grace of His presence.

[1] Cf. B. Elahi, *The Path of Perfection* (PP), chaps III and IV.

Study 1

The Existence of God

Introduction. Arguments for the Existence of God. The Permanence and Universality of the Concept of a Divinity; Necessity of a First Transcendent Cause. **The Obviousness of God**. Potential Faculty of Human Beings for Verifying the Existence of God; Reasons for Atheism.

Introduction

By nature, every individual carries within himself or herself the desire to progress and, above all, to know the unknown. But in order to proceed correctly in the search for spiritual 'knowledge' and to reach real truths, it is of paramount importance to have at one's disposal the axioms and theorems of 'spiritual science' that deal with rights and duties. Therefore, one must first have an overview of such matters as the Creator, Creation, human beings and the process of perfection, all of which form part of the basis of spiritual science. This first study will be devoted to the question of God's existence.

In our minds, the word 'God' has more or less clear overtones; even the atheist who denies God refers to a certain idea of Him. Now, where does this idea come from? Is there a being corresponding to this idea? What is God, really? Is it He who created us and Whom we therefore call the Creator, or is it we humans who have created God?

Arguments for the Existence of God

When we review the history of humanity, we notice that any idea of purely human origin, meaning one that is derived from the imagination of human beings, is bound to disappear sooner or later; eventually, it is simply abandoned and nobody believes in it any longer. But the idea of God, or if you prefer, the idea of a transcendent being, has always existed in the thought of human beings. It has imposed itself upon them as obvious and has resisted all assaults by numerous ideologies which have spoken against it. The great majority of people, if not all of them, have always felt some interest in metaphysical phenomena. The other world, the soul, God, our eternal destiny – all these matters intrigue and fascinate people. In this respect, the idea of the Divine seems to have a consistency which radically sets it apart from any belief that is dependent upon specific cultures, theories or ideologies. There is a permanence and universal character to the idea of God which clearly shows that it is not a creation of human beings, but rather that it originates with them and naturally accompanies them like an imprint.

In any case, common sense tells us that no being can be its own creator, and that nothingness cannot create anything. Thus, there must be a creational cause at the origin of everything, which is as distinct from everything else as it is from nothingness. If we trace the chain of creation from cause to cause, we are forced to stop somewhere and to assume the existence of a first cause[1] – a Creator. Another argument is that no being has the power to create an entity which transcends, or which is superior to, itself. Since human beings are endowed with an intellect and a transcendent will, they have the ability to act against what nature dictates to them, be it the nature around them or their own inner nature. Yet we see that nature cannot help but follow its own course. So we can say that we transcend nature, which therefore cannot be responsible for creating us. Though it is true that simple elements can combine in such a way as to produce something complex (as when simple chemical elements form complex molecule), it is nonetheless difficult to understand how something (nature) could produce out of its own resource something else (a being) which not only transcends it, but also stands up to it.

There are, of course, other arguments in favour of the existence of the Creator, such as those that focus on the order of the universe or the perfection of creation, but what we have just said is sufficient for our purpose. These few reflections are not meant to exhaust the debate on the existence of God. One could always object that these arguments are not proof in the strict sense of the term. However, as soon as we consider human beings in their metaphysical dimension, we cannot deny that a network of presumptions directs us towards the necessary existence of a Creator. God, in fact, does not need to be proven; He is an obvious fact, a self-evident reality that one acknowledges but which cannot be sufficiently proven to those who have not yet developed the faculty of acknowledging it. For how can one prove to someone lacking the sense of sight, that a lamp is lit?

The Obviousness of God

I say that God is self-evident, realizing that the word 'God' bears a troubling or displeasing connotation to some. Yet, whether we like it or not, everything that happens to us has to do with Him. If we are not conscious of this fact, it is because our metaphysical senses are still overshadowed by our body and its physical senses. One cannot deny the existence of air simply by saying, 'I see no air, so I deny its existence.' Likewise, one cannot deny God on the pretext that one does not see Him. Just as the existence of air is verified through its effects or with the aid of special devices, the existence of God is verified through the intermediary of an appropriate faculty which can detect His imprints or signs, and which can even see and hear Him.

Like everything else related to our transcendent reason, this faculty is only potentially present in human beings; to benefit from it, we have the duty to actualize it. It is comparable, for example, to a jeweller's faculty of distinguishing between true and false diamonds. If you show me two diamonds, one genuine and the other false, I would not be able to distinguish which is false, whereas a jeweller could do so at a mere glance. That is because the jeweller sought and was able to develop this faculty. To actualize our faculty of recognizing the imprints of the Creator, a number of conditions must be met. I will mention only two:

• First, we must believe that reality is not limited to the scope of our physical senses. Indeed, if we are not convinced of this fact, we will not even care to develop this faculty.

• Second, we must want to do so. In order to awaken within us the desire to develop this faculty, God always presents us with obvious signs that are likely to create the motivation for us to see Him and to know Him. All of us have had such an experience at least once in our lifetime.

When these two conditions are satisfied, we can gradually develop the power to see God, that is to actualize out that potential faculty. Whoever wants to develop and educate the faculty of knowing his Creator must knock at His door; God makes it incumbent upon Himself to open the door and to extend His hand, and we have the duty to grasp that hand.

God is in everything, everywhere and with everyone. Whether in a dream or while we are awake, directly or indirectly, through the intermediary of His messengers or those who are loved by us, or through any other means – even a passerby in the street – He communicates with each one of us. But in order to hear Him and to understand Him, we must first learn how to decode His messages.

Suppose you are listening to a symphony. The symphony is composed of notes; these notes are played on certain scales; these scales, according to certain patterns, form different modes; these modes serve as a backdrop for melodies; and all the melodies together form the symphony. But only an already trained ear can differentiate between all these elements. In the same way, the divine symphony is constantly being played in everything around us. But to understand the messages of the Creator, we must educate our thought by means of sound principles so that it can gradually develop and attain full maturity.

For the faculty of seeing the imprints or effects of God and of recognizing His signs is dependent upon the degree of maturity of the soul and the alertness of the spiritual sense. Only when our soul reaches maturity (the actualization of its metaphysical potentialities) are we able to distinguish and perceive the imprints and effects of the Creator in everything that exists, whether inside or outside of us. As for those who cannot yet distinguish these divine marks, it may be that their soul is still too young, or that they have been unwilling to set out on the right path, or that their soul is intoxicated and made ill. It should be made clear, however, that the soul's age is independent of biological age; thus, it is possible that one may be physically old but have a soul that has not reached its maturity, and conversely, a person who is physically young may indeed be spiritually mature (Fig. 1). There are also those who possess the maturity that would enable them to know God, but because of certain social and cultural circumstances they refuse to acknowledge the messages of the Creator.

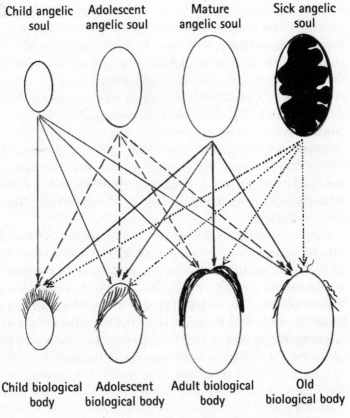

Figure 1   Relationship between the different ages of the soul and the body

Whatever a soul's level of maturity may be, no one can truly deny God's existence, for in every human being the existence of a transcendent will and the voice of his conscience are patent signs of the divine presence. If a person rejects or denies the voice of conscience, then he detests and denies God Himself; but if he loves that voice and believes in it, then, unawares, he loves God and believes in Him. Actually, no one can really ignore God, for no one ignores the voice of his conscience.

Why is it, then, that some people do ignore Him and even go so far as to try to deny His existence? When we examine the major movements or trends of thought denying the existence of God, we realize that the criticisms are in fact directed at the definitions, and more specifically, the interpretations of God as given by some confessions. But these interpretations are often incomplete, and often doctored and distorted by human minds. That is why rational souls, when confronted with seemingly insoluble problems and with questions that lack answers, such as that of divine justice, have come to the conclusion that God does not exist. In fact, it is not God they reject but rather a certain idea or representation of God founded on incorrect interpretations.

There are those who reject the idea of God because appalling actions are committed in His name. But there again, it is not God who is being denied but rather the legitimacy of the individuals who claim that they commit those acts on His behalf. When all is said and done, however, no one who draws closer to his primordial nature can deny the reality of God's existence, and sooner or later, everyone will get close to his primordial nature.

Questions

You spoke about the representations people have made of God. How do you imagine God?

I imagine God in the image of the God of our time.

But what do you mean by the 'God of our time'?

There is only one sun for the Earth, but the effects of its radiance on beings varies depending on the atmospheric conditions and the environment. Similarly, God is unique, but because living conditions and the human intellect progress with the passing of time, if we want to know God, we must look for Him through the prism of our times.

How can we transform an intellectual belief into one which comes from the heart?

By putting into practice a belief based on true principles.

You said that all ideas of purely human origin are bound to disappear. But atheism itself seems to be an idea which has always existed.

According to the law of opposites, one cannot know anything except through its opposite; this is the reason why atheism must exist wherever the idea of God appears.

According to you, the majority of people, if not all of them, are attracted to the divine. But if we look at today's society it seems to be just the opposite.

All ideas progress through fluctuations – that is, through ups and downs. It's the same in spirituality. Today we are passing through a phase of depression. The current spiritual atmosphere is stifling; it debilitates the soul and does not at all favour its development.

You have said that one must actualize a certain faculty in order to recognize the existence of God, yet for certain people the existence of God is an obvious fact from the outset.

It is a law of creation that human beings must acquire everything through their own efforts. The only thing that is given to them is the means of acquiring what they are entitled to. Thus, if someone has the faculty of recognizing God's existence, he must have worked for it before, whether in this life or in previous lives.

What do you mean by 'imprints' of the Creator?

Look at your 'self': you are an imprint of the Creator; the order of the universe is an imprint of the Creator. Wherever you turn, you find an imprint of the Creator.

God sends us clear signs which we must decode. Isn't it a form of superstition to see signs everywhere?

There is a difference between being superstitious and recognizing authentic signs. Superstition is a belief in something which is imaginary, whereas believing in and then looking for divine imprints leads to the verification of obvious facts.

Why doesn't God manifest Himself directly? Isn't there an intention of misleading us in not doing so?

God is such a powerful source of energy that if He were to manifest Himself to us in His real essence, we would immediately be annihilated. God is so great that 'all creatures, possible or extant and from all times, when compared to His greatness are like a molecule of water on the surface of an ocean million times vaster than the planet Earth' [Ostad Elahi]. That is why He has devised the process of perfection: we can gradually develop the capacity to see this infinite energy without being instantly annihilated.

One of the reasons for atheism, as you mentioned, is the appalling acts committed in the name of God. Religious schisms are often at the root of such horrible acts.

Just like everything that is true, religion must also coexist with falsity or pseudo-truths; human beings are free to choose.

Why does God allow religions to branch into so many factions?

One could compare religions to beautiful ripe fruits which dry and rot under the influence of men. When this occurs, God makes a point of handing mankind a new fruit.

How can we say that God exists and is just when we see all the suffering and misfortune that afflict people's lives?

Since human beings are endowed with free will, everything that happens to them, whether good or bad, is in fact the result of their own actions in this life or previous lives. This principle is a product of God's goodness; it is for our own education and perfection that God returns to us the reactions of our actions and intentions. One must look at the world optimistically, for everything that happens to us is full of lessons.

What should one do to have faith in God?

Any person who sincerely and humbly stands before God, and tries to rid his thoughts of all prejudices and asks for faith with all his heart, will receive an answer that will manifest itself through a particular inner warmth; one has to feel this to understand what it is.

To stand before God?

Since God is everywhere, to stand before God means to imagine Him and to really feel that He is present, facing us.

How come so many scientists doubt God's existence?

I think that today's material sciences are still at an embryonic stage. When they develop more fully, the discrepancy between science and true spirituality will vanish.

What do you mean by 'real truths'?

A real truth is a truth that corresponds to an objective truth which can lead us to certitude, that is, to the recognition of its reality.

How can we recognize an idea of purely human origin?

Such an idea has only one dimension and its application brings about only material results, even if it is disguised in a spiritual form. An idea that is of divine origin possesses both dimensions.

You question the interpretations of God presented by certain confessions. But they are almost the only sources that speak of God – can we find Him elsewhere?

In yourself, by yourself.

---

[1] Naturally, an infinite process of creation from cause to cause in the realm of creatures is conceivable in the realm of creatures; it is not strictly speaking illogical. In the same way that one can infinitely divide a segment without ever reaching an 'ultimate' part of it, it might be said that one can review the causal chains in regress from cause to cause without ever reaching the 'first' cause. But even if we consider them to

be infinite, this infinity is only relative; it calls for a more profound reason or cause, a cause beyond all the series of causes, a Cause of all causes.

Study 2

The Divine Attributes and the Utility of Faith

What is God? God According to the Different Religions; The Necessity of Knowing God by Oneself and through His Manifestations. **The Divine Attributes. The Utility of Faith.** Faith is Indispensable to Receiving Divine Warmth and Light; Faith as a Driving Force; The Risks of Disbelief.

In the last study, I tried to show through a few simple and natural chains of reasoning that the idea of God imposes itself upon us as an obvious fact and that He must exist. This study will be devoted to the definition of God and the utility, or benefit, of believing in Him.

What is God?

In order to have an overview of this matter, let us first look in a schematic way at the primary characteristics of God, as postulated by the most common religions.

According to Judaism, God is the creator of the universe. He is unique, omnipotent, incorporeal, omniscient, just, merciful and active. He constantly intervenes in His creation and is concerned with what happens in the world. He appears as an exclusive God because He wants those to whom He manifests Himself to acknowledge Him as sole and unique. In my view, this exclusive character is an educational strategy: God wants to educate human beings, so He commands them to worship Him and only Him.

In Zoroastrianism, the supreme God, Ahura, is the creator and guardian of the cosmic and moral order. He reigns over several divine categories, which in turn preside over definite domains of nature and manifest aspects of the supreme God.

In Hinduism, God the creator is only one of the manifestations of the Absolute or the impersonal Brahman, a God withdrawn into Himself who meditates on the world but who does not actually create it. Gods are numerous in this tradition and are subjected to the rule of Karma. It would require several studies to expound these ideas clearly; this is merely a rough delineation of the matter.

In Buddhism, there is no reference to God or to a supreme creator. However, it is said that one day, sitting in a small Simsapâ forest with a few leaves in his hand, Buddha spoke to his disciples in the following words: 'What I have reveled to you, compared to all the things I know but have not yet unveiled, is like these few leaves in my hand compared to all the leaves in this forest; I have only said that which is necessary for you.' These words seem to indicate that everything has not been said. And as a matter of fact, it is very difficult to believe that a man such as Buddha, who had reached perfection, had not known God.

As for Christianity, God is above all a God of love, represented by the person of Christ. Thus the incarnation and suffering of Christ on the cross are described as a sacrifice by God motivated by love for His creatures; a sacrifice whose aim is to atone for the degradation of the world caused by the original sin. Let us not delve here into the problems posed by the interpretation of the Trinity.

Lastly, according to Islam, God is the creator of all things; He is unique, incorporeal, eternal, transcendent, omnipotent, just etc. He is represented as fearsome for those who deny Him, but He is essentially merciful and generous to those who serve Him and submit to His will.

If we had the original words of the prophets at our disposal, we would realize that there are no fundamental discrepancies among the definitions of God they have provided. Beyond the words of the prophets and saints, however, it is also necessary to try to know God by ourselves, because words alone are incapable of properly conveying what one sees and hears. In fact, to understand the words of the prophets and saints, we must first know God. Someone could spend hours and hours describing a person to us in great detail, but before we actually meet that person all we have is an image created by our own imagination. Nothing can replace actual knowledge of that person. It is the same with knowing of God.

In certain sacred scriptures it is said that God has created human beings in His own image and that He has breathed His Spirit into them. This means several things, including the fact that human beings have the potential to develop the qualities of the divine and to rejoin God. Moreover, and this point deserves particular emphasis, this means that human beings cannot know God except in the image of man. According to the law of causality, every being can come to know God only through the manifestations that are appropriate to his own species, or to the highest species of the planet. For example, if God wants to manifest Himself to a chicken, He will take the form of a human being or that of another chicken. At the time of Christ, those who recognized Him were those who saw the reflection of God in Christ. The Son reflected the Father, and in that sense, the Son and the Father were one and the same person for the people of that time. And yet, God was still 'beyond' His manifestation in the figure of Christ. God manifests Himself universally but relatively to each kind of creature, and thus it is only His manifestations that we can and must seek to know. Only God knows God in the absolute sense – that is, in His essence.

The Divine Attributes

Having taken into account what is written in the sacred scriptures, we are now in a position to define God through His attributes, knowing that the qualities attributed to Him can help us to represent Him to ourselves and to communicate with Him; otherwise, He is indefinable. Ostad Elahi has examined, one by one, all of the divine attributes mentioned in the religious traditions and has come to a synthesis showing how these attributes complement one another without contradiction. Above all, however, he has tried to make sense of those attributes which we have a natural tendency to interpret in an anthropomorphic way, and which we might even be surprised to find among the divine attributes.

God is the creator of the worlds. He primarily appears at the source of what we call 'existence' or 'life'. He is everywhere and with everyone, and He is complete and perfect. He encompasses within Himself all opposites: He is good and merciful, but He has no weakness for anyone. He is sincere with those who are sincere, but He can be a deceiver to those who want to deceive Him. He is very gentle with those who are kind, but very hard on those who consciously defy Him; He neglects those who forget Him, and diverts from the right path those who intentionally divert others from the right path. He strengthens the faith of those who believe in Him, and hardens the convictions of those who deride Him. In fact, He acts exactly like a mirror: He reflects to human beings the effects of their own intentions

– He acts in a base manner towards those who are base and is noble to those who are noble. However, since the basis of creation is generosity, His grace, forgiveness and mercy prevail over His Justice. For example, when He reflects back to human beings their positive actions He multiplies the effects; on the other hand, when He reflects their negative actions, by virtue of His mercy, the reaction is merely equal to the original action. Moreover, if God sends back to human beings the reflection of their own intentions and actions, it is not as a means of revenge but rather it is with an educational and therapeutic aim, for the real God does not have any negative traits rooted in weaknesses such as egoism, jealousy, pettiness, vengeance, greed, tyranny etc. God loves His creatures and constantly looks after them.

We were asking ourselves what God is, and we have provided a sketch of His attributes. But defining God is not enough; we have to understand why we need to believe in Him, or to be more precise, what utility there is for us to believe in God.

The Utility of Faith

We saw in the preliminary study that every being has three universal innate rights at his disposal, one of which was the right of 'attracting benefit and rejecting loss'. For human beings, who are bi-dimensional creatures, these two functions occur automatically[1] in the physical or basharic dimension.[2]

From a metaphysical viewpoint, however, human beings are endowed with an intellect and a transcendent will, so that they must manage these functions on their own, through their own will. Thus, they must learn by themselves to distinguish between what is good and what is bad for them. If our will is not educated and governed by sound and balanced reason – celestial reason – it may very well lead us to make decisions that are contrary to our best interests. This is simply the price we have to pay for our transcendent (metaphysical) dimension.

The germ of celestial reason exists in our real, metaphysical self, but this celestial reason cannot develop harmoniously without two elements: divine warmth and light. Divine warmth is nothing but love for the Divine, the love that we have for our Creator. It is that love which creates in us the motivation and the drive necessary to rejoin Him. Divine light is divine knowledge: all the laws and divine commandments, or if one prefers, all the axioms and theorems established by the Creator and adapted to the nature of our soul.

Now, in order to access the divine warmth and light naturally, it is essential to have faith in the true God, that is, to believe sincerely and firmly in the true God. The true God is the God known in His truth and not as we imagine Him to be; this is the God known and described by the authentic prophets and saints. Believing in a false God, even with complete sincerity, does not give access to genuine divine knowledge. And without access to that knowledge, it is not possible to develop naturally. However, if someone believes in a false God out of ignorance, but in all sincerity and without any material or pseudo-spiritual expectations, God would take it upon Himself to save that person and guide him if he wishes to be guided.

When we speak of growth and development, we immediately think of nutrition. To develop and grow, the soul, like the body, needs appropriate food. This food is precisely the divine light, that is, prescriptions of divine origin, but only to the extent that they are put into practice and assimilated. Again, it is our faith that is the driving force and motivation helping us to conform our actions to divine commandments, until they become our own nourishment. But this raises a question: where do we find this food? The right direction is indicated by the force of attraction that God exerts over all creatures, which is comparable to an electromagnetic force. This force of attraction expresses itself in all beings through an attraction to Him, and in human beings, through faith and love. Thus, the more faith we have and the more we are attracted to Him, and the more we draw nearer to Him, the more this attraction increases and the less likely it becomes that we will deviate from the right direction.

Creatures can be likened to iron filings in that, with the exception of human beings and responsible creatures in general, they are all guided naturally in the right direction merely by the strength of God's prevailing electromagnetic force. Human beings, however, have a transcendent will which affects both the quality of their 'iron filings' and the direction of their motion. If the iron filings rust, the influence of the electromagnetic force diminishes. To avoid fatal deviations, therefore, we must do everything possible to tune our will to the same 'frequency' as that of God's. If we believe in the true God and allow ourselves to be guided by Him, we will naturally take the right direction; we will then have access to divine warmth and light, and consequently we will nourish ourselves with divine instructions.

If we really want to grasp what is lost by not believing in God, it is helpful to distinguish between two cases. Someone who does not believe in God but listens to the voice of his conscience would still benefit – although less fully – from divine warmth and light because he unconsciously believes in God. This person's development is slower than that of someone who actually believes in God, and more importantly, he is extremely fragile when exposed to the trials of life. If a person who does not believe in the true God nevertheless acts morally and follows the biddings of his conscience, he is actually obeying the divine commandments without being aware of it. After a certain period of time – provided that he does not fall – he will eventually come to believe in the true God. On the other hand, someone who neither believes in God nor listens to the voice of his conscience, deprives himself of divine warmth and light.

To illustrate our existential situation, we could compare the the descent of the metaphysical man into the physical body to a fall to the bottom of a very deep ravine. As a result of the 'Original Contract', God has made it incumbent upon Himself to always extend a rope of guidance to those on Earth: this rope has existed since the beginning of humanity and will continue to exist until the very last human being. In order to test us, however, there are necessarily various forces which tempt us by offering their own ropes, and it is up to us to distinguish between the right and the wrong ropes (Fig. 2). If we want to seize the right rope to pull ourselves out of the ravine we have fallen in, we must sincerely believe in the true God; this is one of the primordial duties of human beings. He who believes in a false God is holding on to rope whose end is tied to a shrub. Inevitably, the shrub will eventually be uprooted and he will fall to the bottom of the ravine. He who does not believe in God but who still listens to the voice of his conscience is grasping a rope whose end is tied to a string. It is possible to get out of the ravine this way, but the risk is enormous because as soon as one encounters too strong a temptation, the string will break. He who does not believe in any God, whether true or false, and does not even listen to the voice of his conscience, does not see any rope at all; he will only realize that there was a rope once he reaches the other world, but then it will be too late to grasp it.

The divine rope is present in both worlds, but, with few exceptions, it is no longer possible to grasp it in the other world if one has failed to do so in this world. In fact, although such a person will eventually be able to see the rope and be witness to the happiness of those who have managed to climb out of the ravine and continue their ascent in the other world, the rope will forever remain out of its reach. One can imagine the remorse that such a person feels; it is as if a friend invites you to buy a lottery ticket with him and a few days after having refused you suddenly realize he has hit the jackpot in partnership with another friend. What one feels in such a situation is in fact almost nothing compared to the remorse of those who miss the opportunity to grasp the divine rope in this world. Yet, one should not think that being stricken with remorse is totally in vain, for no suffering that comes from the divine origin is futile for human beings. God is an educator and as a benevolent therapist with his creatures. Thus, among other things, the usefulness of remorse is that it makes us mature in such a way that next time we will not repeat the same mistakes.

To conclude, let us emphasize that God always extends His hand to us. However, because we have a free will, it is our responsibility to grasp that hand. Some people say, 'If God exists, why doesn't He show Himself to us?' But have these people really taken a step towards Him? God always answers the call of those who know how to call Him and truly make the effort to go in His direction. And the nearer we get to Him, the more we feel His help, the more we are filled with His love.

Questions

You have mentioned the true God, but it is a fact that all religions do not define God in the same way. How can we get to know that true God?

To know the true God, we must avoid fashioning Him after our own model; we should, on the contrary, fashion ourselves after His. What prevents us from knowing the true

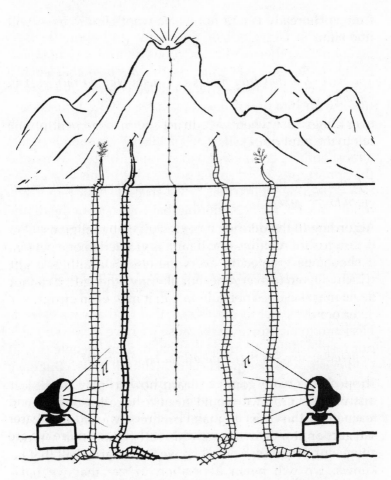

Figure 2   *'God has made it incumbent upon Himself always to extend a rope of guidance to those on Earth, but in order to test us, there are necessarily various forces which tempt us by offering their own ropes'*

God is our pride: we are so proud of our intellectual knowledge and material achievements that we disregard that little door which can show us the way to the true God. Someone who sincerely looks for the true God – that is,

God as He really is and not as we want Him to be – will find Him.

You have said that iron filings can rust. Why do they rust in human beings?

Iron filings rust when we entrust the management of our self to the imperious self.

Is faith a gift in the same sense as artistic or literary talent, or is it given to everyone?

According to the definition of God given by religions, God is Just. Justice requires that if faith is granted to one person, it should be granted to everyone else. So, faith is a gift which is given to everyone, but like any other gift, it cannot develop if one does not cultivate it; it may even atrophy or deteriorate.

How can we develop the divine attributes within us?

Suppose we were going to learn how to play a musical instrument. First, we would need to take lessons from a teacher, and in order to make progress, we must seek his satisfaction, for it is through his satisfaction that we can gauge our progress. And when we have learned all that he knows, we will be in a position to say that we have 'reached his music'.

In the same way, if we want to acquire divine qualities, we must seek God's satisfaction. To do so, however, it is essential that He educates us; in other words, that He teaches us what to do and what not to do. This is the reason He has sent us, through His messengers, prescriptions and instructions which we must follow if we wish to acquire His qualities.

Putting into practice principles of purely human origin

cannot lead us towards our goal. On the contrary, they may even give us complexes and repressions that impede our progress. To develop the divine qualities, an imperative condition is to know and to believe in the original and fundamental principles which bear the divine seal, and to practise the ethics and morals of divine origin. This idea of the divine seal is fundamental: it is what distinguishes the authentic religion from merely human ideologies, and doctrines and systems that borrow their principles and prescriptions from here and there. An authentic religion must be set forth by one who has a mission, and it must bear the divine seal.

But how can we judge whether God is satisfied with us?

In the beginning, it is difficult to detect the signs of God's satisfaction by ourselves. The smallest step that we take on a divine path appears to us as significant and fills us with pride, which falsifies our judgment. If we have the opportunity of getting close to an authentic divine person, God informs us about His satisfaction through him. As we move further along the path of perfection, we gradually learn to thwart the trickeries of our imperious self, especially our pride, and our judgment becomes more reliable.

Which principles must we observe to obtain God's satisfaction?

The first principle is to feel concerned with and to be conscious of the importance of what is at stake. Unfortunately, we do not feel concerned about the hereafter and with eternal life, and even though we will not escape them.

The second principle is to believe in the true God.

The third principle is to believe in the fact that our real 'self' is eternal, and that life does not end with physical death.

The fourth principle is to believe in the fact that our intentions and actions are recorded, and that in the next world, we will reap what we have sown here: hence the importance of this terrestrial and temporal life for our eternal destiny.

The fifth principle is to put ethical and moral prescriptions into practice until they become second nature. For example, one of the principal commandments is to know and respect our own rights and duties, as well as those of others.

On the one hand, you say that one must know God by what the prophets and saints have said about Him, but on the other hand, you stress the importance of personal knowledge.

Authentic prophets and saints, and more generally, those we can call divine persons, communicate to us authentic divine principles and, in some cases, correct our mistakes. But the acquisition, assimilation and practical application of these principles is up to us. The divine beings can teach us what the divine attributes are, but it is up to us to learn and to understand them.

When we say that God is just, are we not in a way attributing typically human feelings to Him?

God can have everything. Since He is dealing with me, why shouldn't He have human feelings? When you are talking to a two- or three-year-old child, you do not put on a serious air or talk to him as you would with an adult; you bring yourself down to the child's level and start talking as he does. In the same way, when God speaks to me, He brings Himself down to my level; He talks and thinks just like me – otherwise, I would not be able to understand Him.

You emphasized the idea of a natural development of the real self. Are you implying that there is such a thing as artificial development?

The application of the principles created by the Creator, which are adapted to the nature of our angelic soul, brings about a harmonious and natural growth of the soul. But when one embarks on pseudo-spiritualities and applies various techniques to develop, more or less rapidly, certain powers or altered states (such as the ability to levitate or other paranormal powers), this entails artificial development of one part of the self at the expense of the others.

You have said that in order to test us, there have to be various forces for tempting us. Why should human beings have to be tested?

It is a necessity of the spiritual path.

There are many things you said which are not really new. Could you please tell us what is different about Ostad Elahi, and in what sense his system of thought is different from syncretism?

Not only did Ostad Elahi have extensive knowledge of theology and philosophy, but he was also engaged in practical spiritual research and practice. He assessed the authentic principles of religions and reconstituted the missing links of the chain which leads us to the understanding of the purpose of human beings. Theory alone is insufficient in spirituality: experience and practice are also needed, and it is in these fields that Ostad Elahi managed to discover the missing links.

Generally speaking, religious syncretism produces a contradictory ensemble which cannot answer questions it raises by itself. Ostad Elahi's way of thought – I know this for a fact – is a harmonious whole which is devoid of contradictions. But to assess it, one must experience it for oneself.

---

[1] For example, the digestive system automatically selects the ingredients which are necessary for the body.

[2] From *bashar*, a term of Arabic origin referring to the human being as a species. It is used here to designate the animal dimension in human beings; the bashar is thus the human being minus its angelic soul, or in other words, the human being considered as a human animal.

Study 3

The Story of Creation

Creation according to Sacred Texts and Science.
Genesis; Creation According to the Koran; The
'Big Bang'. **The Story of Creation by Ostad
Elahi. Some Directions for Reflection.**

The theme of this third study is Creation. Although human
beings have always studied this subject, the question of
Creation remains an enigmatic and seemingly insoluble
problem.

Before approaching the subject of Creation through the
thoughts of Ostad Elahi, I will briefly present a survey of
what has been said about it in the most famous religious
texts. I will also discuss the manner in which science deals
with this question today.

Creation according to Sacred Texts and Science

In the book of Genesis,[1] it is said:

> In the beginning God created the heaven and the earth. And
> the earth was without form, and void; and darkness was upon
> the face of the deep. And the Spirit of God moved upon the
> face of the waters.

According to Genesis, Creation was completed in six days, and the seventh day was the day of rest.

On the first day God said, 'Let there be light': and there was light [. . .] And God called the light Day, and the darkness he called Night . . .

On the second day God said, 'Let there be a firmament in the midst of the waters, and let it divide the waters from the waters' [. . .] And God made the firmament, and divided the waters which were under the firmament from the waters which were above the firmament: and it was so.

On the third day God said, 'Let the waters under the heaven be gathered together unto one place, and let the dry land appear': and it was so. And God called the dry land earth; and the gathering together of the waters called he seas: and God saw that it was good. And God said, 'Let the earth bring forth grass, the herb yielding seed, and the fruit tree yielding fruit after his kind, whose seed is in itself, upon the earth': and it was so.

On the fourth day God said, 'Let there be lights in the firmament of the heaven to divide the day from the night; and let them be for signs, and for seasons, and for days, and years: And let them be for lights in the firmament of the heaven to give light upon the earth': and it was so. And God made two great lights; the greater light to rule the day, and the lesser light to rule the night: he made the stars also.

On the fifth day God said, 'Let the waters bring forth abundantly the moving creature that hath life, and fowl that may fly above the earth in the open firmament of heaven'. And God created great whales, and every living creature that moveth, which the waters brought forth abundantly, after their kind, and every winged fowl after his kind: and God saw that it was good.

On the sixth day God said, 'Let the earth bring forth the living creature after his kind, cattle, and creeping thing, and beast of the earth after his kind': and it was so. And God made the beast of the earth after his kind, and cattle after their kind, and every thing that creepeth upon the earth after his kind: and God saw that it was good.

In the second story of the Creation, it is said:

> And the Lord God formed man of the dust of the ground, and breathed into his nostrils the breath of life; and man became a living soul [. . .] and he took one of his ribs, and closed up the flesh instead thereof. And the rib, which the Lord God had taken from man, made he a woman, and brought her unto the man.

In the New Testament, the Creation is also mentioned in a sentence which is probably one of the most well-known in the Bible:

> In the beginning was the Word, and the Word was with God, and the Word was God [. . .] and the Word was made flesh, it lived among us and we contemplated it in His glory.[2]

In the verses of the Koran[3] which deal with the Creation, it is said:

> Your Lord is God, and He created the heavens and the earth, and whatever stands in between, in six days.

> The heavens and the earth formed a compact mass and He separated them.

> His throne was on the water.

> He created the earth in two days.

> Then He turned towards the sky which was a smoke [. . .] He settled the seven heavens in two days

> It is He who created day and night, the sun and the moon, each of them moving about in its own orbit.

> He raised the heavens without any visible columns.

> We have created every living creature out of water.

> We had water come down from the heavens and We raised on earth all sorts of useful species.

> It is He who laid out the earth, placed mountains and rivers on it; He placed two couples of every fruit.

He has propagated all sorts of animals.

We have created the heavens, the earth and all things in between according to Right.[4]

Yes, We have created all things according to a decree.

Two points should be emphasized here. The first is that all of creation is founded upon the principle of Right. The second involves the use of the word 'decree'. From a legal point of view, a decree implies action by an executive power within the framework of a constitution, which itself implies the existence of a government. This analogy is indicative of the nature of divine action.

God is the one that created seven heavens and did the same for the Earth. The commandment is brought in them so that you may come to know that God is truly omnipotent and that His knowledge spreads over everything.

Remember that God said to the Angels: 'I am going to create man out of a malleable clay. When I have given him a harmonious form and when I have blown something of My spirit in him, you shall prostrate yourselves before him.'[5]

Let me just briefly remind you of the 'big bang' theory, a view which is now held by the majority of scientists. According to this theory, the universe was created approximately 15 billion years ago from an infinitesimal but expanding original point called 'hypersphere'. The density of energy and the temperature were so high in that point that matter did not exist there, except in the form of radiance and light. In the beginning, the expansion of the hypersphere occurred at prodigious speed, which explains why it has been compared to an explosion and given the suggestive name of 'big bang'.

The Story of Creation by Ostad Elahi

Before moving on to the story of Creation as told by Ostad Elahi, I would like to make a preliminary remark. We are all concerned with our future, whether consciously or not. Scientists are making great efforts to acquire knowledge of the laws of nature in order to help us master it and thereby quell our anxiety, but we should know that sooner or later we will be coping with the demands of the spiritual worlds; when this happens, it will be with the same concern we currently have for our future, along with a feeling of remorse and regret for not having 'understood' sooner.

Now the spiritual worlds are much vaster than the material world, and they, too, are ordered and organized in a very precise manner, being governed by specific and inescapable laws. But what science can deal with these laws? Here, we may speak of a science of spiritual matters, or if you prefer, a spiritual science. However, it would be a mistake to think that these two worlds are independent and separate realms, for it is only in this material world that we can acquire the basic knowledge that will serve as the foundation and cornerstone of our spiritual edifice while, at the same time, serving us as beacons of salvation in the other world.

The following account of the Creation may seem like a product of mere imagination. In fact, however, it contains genuine spiritual axioms and theorems of what we have called 'natural' spiritual science. One could compare this science with Euclidean geometry, which is rooted in non-tangible principles devoid of concrete existence. According to geometry, a point has no dimensions. Now, from the point of view of physical reality, an object without dimensions is non-existent. And yet, a line is an infinite set of 'juxtaposed' points. Since human beings have believed in and accepted such axioms, they have reached tangible and concrete results. On the basis of the science of geometry, they have built monuments, bridges and roads. And all these achievements rest, so to speak, upon points which to us seem non-existent. In the same way, true spiritual axioms and theorems are not immediately tangible for a mind that is not awake yet. But in order to obtain concrete results and to build our spiritual edifice, it is necessary first to discover these axioms, which is nowadays exceedingly difficult, if not impossible. Then, one must firmly believe in them, and more importantly, apply them judiciously.

Ostad Elahi starts the story of Creation[6] with a tribute to the Creator:

All universes belong to Him, but He belongs to nothing and no one. He is without equal; He knows no birth and no death; He is invisible and no one can know His essence. He has granted prophetic missions to all His messengers and has entrusted them with the task of guiding people in their own language. He has allowed me to contemplate the spiritual worlds and has given me the mission of revealing the divine secrets and educating human beings.

Then he goes on to say:

The writings and their interpretations are too scholarly and enigmatic, and they are beyond the understanding of people. So I have tried to express their profound meaning as clearly as possible.

My name is Nur Ali.[7] Since my early childhood, I have been practising mystical asceticism with my father, Haj Nemat, in order to cover all the different spiritual stages assigned to mankind. I am now 29 years old and have come to the end of the stage called 'God in God'. Until now, I have not passed a single moment with my thought detached from the Divine, and I have continuously lived in His Light, His Love, and in the hope of His Clemency.

One day, deep in my thoughts, I found myself suddenly overwhelmed by His manifestation and was carried away. I found myself in another universe. In that spiritual universe,

I was taken in to an assembly called the 'Assembly of the Saviours'. As soon as I was introduced, their superior welcomed me with a compassionate expression in his eyes. The Creation and the laws of the universe were revealed to me in the following way. Everyone is free to accept it or not.

God is the Creator of all creatures. No one knows where He resides; He is the only One who knows Who and What He is. He planned the creation of the universes. This plan, which is the basis of the totality of beings and realities, became the Quiddity and the primordial matter. Set in an indefinable place, in a form which was not comparable to any other, and of a colour that had no colour, the whole thing resembled pure water. But it was not water – and it was perpetually moving in an infinite and colourless space. The Quiddity had come into existence from the reflection of God, and the primordial matter had come into existence from the reflection of the Quiddity. This whole was beyond all imagination, and the Quiddity moved about in this spiritual space.

Suddenly, a voice coming from God made itself heard by the Quiddity: 'Reflect upon your origin and know your God [. . .] You are the being from which the totality of all possibilities comes into existence, for all power, all might, as well as everything that is in you comes from me.' The Quiddity said: 'If You are with me, why do I not see You?' The Voice replied: 'As long as you cannot see yourself, you will not see Me, and as long as you do not know yourself, you will not know Me.'

Then the Voice said: 'Blaze up within yourself!' The Quiddity became all aflame within itself and was transported with ecstasy. When the Quiddity came to, wherever it looked all was black. But in the heart of this blackness, which was called 'darkness', a light like the sun now broke through the obscurity [Fig. 3].

Those luminous rays emanating from the Quiddity were all that appeared in the heart of this blackness. The original space in which the Quiddity moved was all light. That light, however, could not reveal itself in light; there had to be darkness for it to appear. That is the reason why light and darkness must coexist, in all situations.

Again said the Voice: 'As long as there was no darkness,

*Figure 3   'But in the heart of this blackness, which was called
"darkness", a light like the sun broke through the obscurity'*

your own image could not appear; for the same reason, you
must have some corporeality to see My image within yourself.
For corporeality is like darkness, and that is why your own
image is visible in that darkness.'

The Quiddity asked: 'How should I find that corporeality?
Isn't this light corporeality?' And the Voice replied: 'That light
is an emanation of your spirit. But what I mean by "body" is
the corporeal "covering" which must extend from yourself to
all others. So you must again blaze up within yourself, so that
everything that is not you may separate from you and return to
its own self. For that which is not from you has been created by
My imagination and I have made you to be its cause. Now
blaze up within yourself!'

On God's command, the Quiddity became all enflamed
within itself. Suddenly, he heard the sound of a terrible

explosion and something like smoke, like mist or like dust and soot, obscured its vision. Then in an 'instant'[8] its view was clear again, and it saw that there was no longer any trace of that darkness or of the radiant light which had emanated from its being.

In that infinite blue space[9] which was its own, the Quiddity saw nothing but its companions; and in addition, he gazed upon three other infinite spaces, in each of which there was also a small assembly. Each spiritual space had its own colour. One was the colour of fire, but it did not burn. Another was the colour of the wind, but it was not of wind. The third was the colour of the earth, verdant and pleasing, but without the materiality of the earth. In each of these three infinite spiritual spaces there appeared many different particles, big and small, more or less luminous, with their colour and nature corresponding to their space, and all in perpetual motion [Fig. 4].

In these three spaces, the particles were created in pairs (male and female), and they constituted the souls of the totality of all creatures. In the blue colour space, there was nothing but the Quiddity and its companions. Beyond these spaces, which were home to the souls, the Quiddity saw innumerable planets and stars. The planets were big or small, luminous or dark, cold or warm etc. Each of them had its own particular colour and configuration and each was different from the others.

On each inhabited planet, depending on their proper natural conditions, there existed different creatures of various forms and species, in pairs of male and female, with the same shapes and structures that we may encounter today. But there were all bodies without life and forms without souls, because their souls were located in the three spiritual spaces already mentioned, and God had not yet given the order for the souls to join bodies.

Among the creatures of each inhabited planet was one noble and superior species which had power and dominion over the others. That is why on Earth human beings have dominion over all creatures.

God said to the Quiddity: 'You are the mirror of My Being; you reflect My Power and My Thought.'

After having explained to the Quiddity the reason for all of

Figure 4   The Quiddity and the three spiritual spaces

the creatures, God said to him: 'Signal all the souls to descend into their corresponding bodies, so that the universe may begin to turn and begin to reproduce.'

And the Quiddity, following the divine command, did signal, but the souls did not descend into their bodies. Then God said: 'In order for the souls to enter bodies, your image and that of your companions should be reflected on the planets.'

As soon as the souls saw the light of the Quiddity and its companions, they went into ecstasies and they descended into the bodies. The creatures of the planets, who had been lifeless, took life and multiplied.

Some Directions for Reflection

What should we think of this story? At first glance, it might seem to be just another cosmogonic or poetic myth, but in fact it conceals teachings, spiritual axioms and theorems with extremely precise meanings. The following are some of the essential points that have been considered in the course of this study; they can provide some directions for further reflection.

The Creation was made gradually. There is a progression in creation. Consequently, just as the scientists say, creation was achieved step by step. In that sense, one could say there is no contradiction between evolution and creation: creation itself is a process.

God has created human beings in His own image. Human beings have the potential of becoming God-like, meaning the potential to acquire the divine qualities.

The Word became flesh. For us to benefit from the divine presence and teaching, and eventually attain a state of bliss, it is necessary that God takes human form.

The Creation is based on right. This means, among other things, that as soon as a being is created – emerging from nothingness and coming into existence – it is endowed with certain rights. Thus everyone must know these rights, must claim and defend them, while also respecting the rights of others. We have the right to survive, the right to pursue our life and the right to reach the eternal felicity for which we have been created. We have the right, then, to be guided in the same way as the people who lived at the time of the great prophets and knew them. And according to our intentions and actions, whether individual or collective, God makes it incumbent upon Himself to give us what we are entitled to.

God created seven heavens and He did the same for the Earth. This means that there are levels of proximity to the Divine Entity for the beings and for the planets. Some planets are superior to others; one might say that seven levels of proximity exist for the planets, and that these levels also have some influence on creatures.

Reflect upon your origin and know your God. This applies to all of us: we must return to our origin, we must refer to that origin, which is to say that we must know God. This is what is called the 'Contract'. The representatives of mankind have entered into an original contract with God: the descendants of human beings have the right to be guided, and God must guide them. The coming of His messengers is a part of that contract; they had to come, and they will continue to come again and again until we eventually arrive safe and sound.

As long as you shall not know yourself, you shall not know Me. Ostad Elahi says elsewhere: 'Delve within yourself to know God; by knowing God you shall know everything.' What is the meaning of 'delving within oneself'? To better understand this, let us take the example of medicine. To diagnose an illness, a physician 'delves within himself'; in other words, he intensely reflects and meditates upon the symptoms he has observed. But for this meditation to be effective and fruitful, it first requires a correct theoretical and practical knowledge of medicine, as well as a real understanding and assimilation of this knowledge on the part of the physician. Things are the same in spirituality. If one wants to know oneself, so as to know God and the whole universe, one must delve within oneself. And delving within oneself implies both a knowledge of correct spiritual principles and a practice of those principles in order to assimilate them. Then, on the basis of observation, one can delve within oneself, meditate and understand. We thus delve more and more deeply within ourselves until our reflection, or our meditation, becomes more profound and our spiritual understanding develops. When we know ourselves, we know God.

Lastly, since we are concerned with founding a science of spirituality, here is a spiritual axiom I would like to submit for your reflection: '*God* + *era x* = *God of era x*.' An obvious application of this principle is that if God exists, and we live in our own particular era, then God must always manifest Himself and act towards us as the '*God of our era*'. It has always been and will always be like that; hence the general formula, which is valid for every era.

Questions

You said that 'the Word was made flesh', meaning that God was made Man. I understand that you consider Jesus to be God.

I said that it was necessary for God to take a human form, to manifest Himself as a human being in order to be access-ible to humans. Sometimes He manifests Himself totally in one person; sometimes only partially. Jesus was one of His manifestations. There were other manifestations before him and after him, and there will continue to be manifest-ations until the end of time. Very often, they are only known by a few people during their own lifetime, but their teachings are transmitted and spread to all of humanity. Some of them, such as Christ, also had the mission to reveal who they were, but the majority of them remain unknown.

What difference do you draw between techniques for spiritual meditation and the meditation in which one delves within oneself?

Delving within oneself is a gradual process which accompanies the natural maturation of the self and the progressive development of spiritual understanding. Gradually, the 'viator'[10] turns his eyes away from others and looks within, in the sense that he sees, for example, his own faults rather than those of others, or that he sees the cause of his troubles in himself rather than in others. Step by step, one level at a time, he delves within himself, learns to know himself and feels more and more humble. Delving within oneself does not mean withdrawing into oneself; on the contrary, it is a mode of thought which is to be practised at every moment, whether one is alone or in the midst of society.

Meditation techniques also allow one to delve within oneself, but in an artificial and premature manner, without developing any spiritual understanding. Used as a technique for relaxation or concentration, this kind of meditation can be very beneficial, but as far as spirituality is concerned, such techniques turn out to be deviating and dangerous for immature souls.

Do you think that God is present in all creation?

God is present in every being, just as the point is present in every geometrical shape. It is the presence of God within each of us that makes us go towards Him: the Christian, the Muslim, the pagan, the idolater, the atheist etc. – all go towards God, each in his own particular way. But when you manage to find the God of your time, your progress is much faster. It's like someone who uses modern transportation: he will progress much faster than those using archaic modes of travel.

What is the use of knowing how creation began?

If you want to know where you are going, you must know where you have come from.

[1] The King James Bible, Genesis, 1: 1–3. The Torah, Genesis.

[2] Gospel of St John, Prologue, 1: 1–16.

[3] In the Koran, when God speaks to Mohammad, He refers to Himself either through the plural form of the first person ('We created all living things from water') or through the singular form of the third person ('Say [to men]: Your Lord is God').

[4] Right (*haqq*) is that which is without deviation, which does not depart from the rule; it is moral rectitude and integrity; it is also synonymous with equity and justice, to which the ideas of merit and compensation are related; it also means whatever is legitimate, whatever one is entitled to claim (and this applies to members of society as well as to living creatures such as animals, plants or minerals). The first creation of God, from whom all other creatures are derived, is also called 'Right', which is why all creation can be said to rest upon the principle of Right.

[5] Suras VII:54; XXI:30; XI:7; XLI:11–12; XXI:33; XXXI:10; XIII:2–3; XXXI:10; XLVI:2; LIV:49–50; LXV:12 (translations by the author).

[6] *Khashf ol-Haqâieq* (Unveiling of the Truth), unpublished manuscript, 1924.

[7] Ostad Elahi's forename.

[8] 'Instant' here does not mean that infinitely short period of time which corresponds to our earthly experience of time: if one wanted to measure that 'instant' with our devices, it might well turn out to be millions of years.

[9] The infinity of these spaces is to be understood in a relative sense: it is infinite for us, infinite in relation to creatures, not in relation to God, who is the only thing that can be described as absolutely infinite.

[10] 'Voyager' or 'traveller', from the Latin *via* (path) – anyone pursuing a divine path.

Study 4

The Principles of Creation

The Organization of Creation. The Causal Universe: The Cosmos, The Interworld and The Spiritual Worlds; The Metacausal Universe; The Nine Heavens; The Necessary Principles of Creation: The Principles of Causality, Essence and Existence, Matter and Form, The Process of Perfection, The Rotational Movement and the Translational Movement. **The Purpose behind Creation. Some Directions for Reflection.**

The Organization of Creation

Two universes are to be distinguished in creation: the causal universe and the metacausal universe. The causal universe is made up of the whole cosmos (the physical world), the interworld and the spiritual worlds (the causal spiritual worlds) that are below the level of perfection;[1] all of them are subject to the law of causality. The metacausal universe, on the other hand, is not subject to this law of causality: it is beyond it. The metacausal universe is the seat of the Divine Entity, that is, of all the beings that have rejoined God (Fig. 5).

The whole universe (causal and metacausal) is organized into nine heavens:

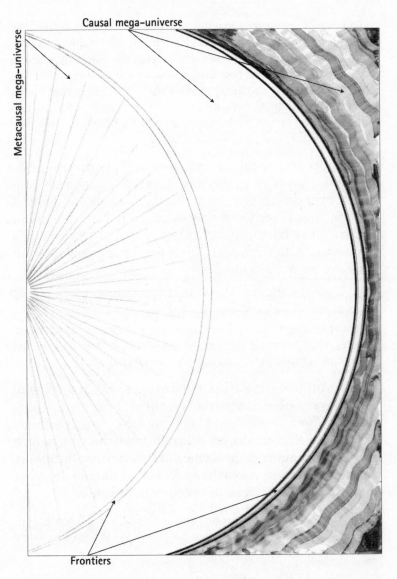

Figure 5   The Universes

The causal universe is located along seven celestial strata. The eighth and ninth heavens are the Throne. The planets are located throughout the first seven heavens: the closer they are to the eighth and ninth heavens, the more eminent they are; the further they are, the more inferior they are. The planet Earth, like many other planets, is located in the first heaven, which is the lowest level. The interworld of every planet is located in the atmosphere of that planet.[2]

All creation is organized and governed by precise laws. One could say that everything in creation has been conceived by a perfect craftsman, for there is not the slightest imperfection, disorder or flaw in creation. Even the tiniest being cannot be conceived better than it is, or situated somewhere better than it is. Thus, everything one observes in nature is simply perfect.

Creation is governed by infallible laws and is based on the following necessary principles:[3] the principle of causality, the principle of essence and existence, the principle of matter and form, the principle of the process of perfection and the principle of rotational and translational movement.[4]

The first principle is the principle of causality, according to which 'every phenomenon or event has a cause', 'nothing occurs without a cause', and 'to know something is to know it by its cause'. The concept of natural determinism, which is at the core of modern science, rests on this principle of causality: every phenomenon can be considered an effect and thus explained by or deduced from its cause.

Creation is founded upon and governed by the law of causality. Only He does not need a cause: He is the cause of all causes [the Necessary Being].[5]

Creation was thus achieved through the law of causality, and everything that exists has a cause. This implies that if we want to obtain anything, we must necessarily go through the appropriate causes.

The second principle is the pair essence/existence, which states that everything that exists necessarily has an essence which precedes it. Essence is what constitutes the permanent and universal nature of something; existence[6] is that which comes out of nothingness, that which is opposed to nothingness. In reality, essence is nothing other than the effect or imprint of God in a being, that is, the presence of God in a being. And it is that presence which enables things to exist and sustains them in their existence.

One can only deal with the imprints of God, because His essence *per se* remains unknowable. To make Himself known, He has created from His substance the Quiddity as well as the primordial matter of all creatures. We are thus permeated with God; we live because He lives within us, and whenever God takes back His effect or imprint from a being, that being immediately ceases to exist. God is the primary and ultimate principle of all things that exist, and His imprint is the essence which is inseparable from everything that exists. We are surrounded by God, we are immersed in God; we are living in God.

One of the effects of God's imprint in beings is movement, and the least perceptible form of life is the transubstantial movement or the essential[7] movement.

As long as there is no divine effect in a being, it cannot come into existence. Existence and the transubstantial movement of every being originate from that divine effect.[8]

Creatures are always in movement, but this is a transubstantial movement. Transubstantial movement animates the whole universe; it is related to the essential and absolute movement of God, and it is what we call the direct link (between the creature and God). The indirect link goes through the chain of causality. The transubstantial movement can be traced in minerals, plants, animals and generally speaking, in every being. [. . .] The transubstantial movement is comparable to respiration in human beings. If one cannot breathe, one dies; similarly, if a creature is deprived of its transubstantial movement, it returns to nothingness. [. . .] The transubstantial movement is the phenomenon which explains why our 'self' does not disappear.[9]

The third necessary principle of creation is the pair matter/form. In the causal universe, matter does not exist without form, and no form exists without matter. Matter is the substratum, whether 'abstract'[10] or not, and with infinite degrees of subtlety, which must necessarily be defined by a form in order to be understood by and to be tangible for creatures. Even souls are made of matter, although it is a very subtle form of matter, infinitely more subtle than the kind our body is made of. Form is thus what defines matter.

The fourth principle is the process of perfection. The path of perfection includes a descending curve, a point of appearance and an ascending curve. Beginning from their initial appearance, beings[11] embark on a journey that ultimately brings them back to their source, which we call the ascending curve or the process of perfection.

> Every being comes into existence from the cause which precedes it and so on, until the last being. This part of the path is called the descending curve. From its point of appearance onwards, every being starts its process of perfection and gradually draws closer to God, eventually rejoining Him. This return to the Source is called the ascending curve.[12]
>
> In principle, all creatures are moving towards their perfection. The human body also perfects itself. Thus, its nervous system is more developed today than it was at the time of our ancestors; all this happens according to a pre-established order and specific rules, not in an anarchic manner.[13]

The fifth principle involves the pair rotational movement/translational movement. '*The rotational movement is the essential movement of each person from his birth to his death.*'[14] It is this movement which allows an individual to maintain his terrestrial identity during his entire life despite undergoing continuous transformations. *'To date, no two individuals have ever been found to have identical fingerprints. It is a well-known fact that the constitutive tissue comprising these fingerprints is constantly changing, yet the patterns remain the same.'*[15] The rotational movement is what makes the tissue change without altering the pattern or 'identity'.

'The change of "garments" corresponds to the translational movement.'[16] When a person leaves this life, abandons his body and arrives in the interworld, he is given a new life if he has yet to finish; this change of terrestrial identity corresponds to the translational movement. Without the rotational movement, the translational movement could not take place.

The Purpose behind Creation

Until we raise the question of the purpose behind creation, it is senseless to know how creation was made and what principles it follows. Ostad Elahi states:

> The purpose behind creation is for every being to reach eternal bliss. The indispensable condition for reaching this goal is to know God. Indeed, as long as we do not know God, we are deprived of total concrete consciousness, and without total concrete consciousness, how can we speak of eternal bliss?

And to the question: 'But how can we come to know God?' he answers:

> Someone who wants to focus his attention on the creation of the universe must first focus on himself, because what has been granted to the universe and to all beings has also been granted to him; when he knows himself, he necessarily knows the One who has given him this 'self', and when he knows God, nothing remains unknown to him.[17]

Thus, the purpose behind creation is for every being to benefit from the Divine Grace. If I were a very generous person I would wish to give, but if there was nobody to whom I could express my generosity, and if at the same time I had the power to create, I would have created someone. The prophet Mohammad reported these words from God: 'I was like a hidden treasure; I wished to be known. I created the creatures in order to be known, in order for you to know Me.'[18] At first we might think that it is rather selfish to say 'I wished to be known'. But if we reflect on the meaning of this phrase, we will understand that attaining knowledge of God is in fact the key to attaining total knowledge, and thus absolute felicity and freedom. The goal of creation, then, is to benefit from all the treasures the Creator has put at the disposal of His creatures.

Some Directions for Reflection

To conclude, I would like to draw your attention once again to a number of points for practice and reflection, since the aim of these studies is neither to speculate nor to produce imaginary theories – even well-reasoned and reasonable ones. Rather, it is to define some principles or guidelines for practical conduct which hopefully will be of some use for our eternal life.

Does peace really exist in the causal world? When we speak of 'peace', we mean absolute peace, which is not in any way comparable to the kind of peace we imagine.

What can we do to know how to behave properly in the causal spiritual world? If we do not learn our duties here, do not think that we will know them any better once we leave our body and reach the other world. No, when we reach the other world, we will be the same person as before and we will have to face the same situations, the only difference being that our body will be made of a more subtle kind of matter. Consequently, if we do not learn our duties here, we will commit faults and make mistakes over there for which we will suffer even more than we would have suffered here, because in the other world, we are more awake and more conscious than in this world.

To know something is to know it by its cause. At the time when the cause of typhoid fever was unknown, people imagined that jinns or demons had entered the sick person's stomach. In the Middle Ages, some surgeons had spiders crawl across their patients' stomachs to cure the fever. This continued until it was discovered that the origin of typhoid fever was simply a bacterium called Eberth's Bacillus. To know something is thus to know it by its cause, and if we want to 'know', we first have to know our primordial cause. If we manage, step by step, to reach our primordial cause, we will know everything.

The presence of God in the being. I am breathing because God is breathing; we are alive because God is within us; we are thinking because God is thinking within us; when we walk, we walk in God.

It is up to us to provide our rotational movement with the right direction. Minerals, plants and animals are determined by the Creator – that is, the direction of their movement is predetermined by Him. But a human being, because of the slight freedom that he has, must direct his transubstantial movement by himself. If he directs it wrongly, who knows where he will end up?

Perfection is achieved progressively. To the question: 'Why did God make the Creation in six days and not in an instant?', Ostad Elahi answers: '*To show that everything in the realm of creation is achieved in a gradual, progressive way. Besides, these six days refer to the "days" during which He created beings; they are not the same kind of days we have on Earth because they are not based on the solar system.*'[19] Consequently, both creation and the return to the Source are necessarily progressive processes, as is the process of perfection.

Questions

You have been speaking about the interworld, the causal spiritual worlds and the causal cosmos. What do you mean by the 'interworld'?

The interworld is the world that is located between each planet and the causal spiritual worlds. It is the provisional residence of souls who have not reached the deadline for their perfection.

Among the necessary principles, you alluded to a somewhat unsettling concept: abstract or subtle matter.

Apart from God and those who have acquired the quality of God, meaning those who have reached perfection, all beings have matter. In the material world, matter is dense, as in a pen, a chair or even our body. But in the interworld, matter is more subtle. The more subtle matter is, the more imperceptible it is to our physical senses, the more concrete it is, and the more penetrating its effect. However, one cannot feel 'abstract' matter without the appropriate senses. Thus, the closer we come to the centre of all reality, the more real, concrete and beautiful everything becomes; conversely, the further away we move from that centre, the less concrete, real and beautiful things are (like our terrestrial world).

You have mentioned the principles which are necessary for creation, especially the principle of causality. Later, you said that the world of the perfect beings was not subject to causality. Does this mean that perfect beings are not a part of creation?

No, this only means that they have developed the divine quality, which itself is not material. They are only pure essence, free from matter and thus from causality. But they can take on any form or matter they wish. Compared to the causal world, they are immaterial; only He is absolutely immaterial.

They can become human again?

Of course. You can even see the reflection of God or a perfect being in a bird, a tree or a stone.

Concerning peace, you just said that the kind of peace we attain in this world is not an absolute peace.

Exactly. It is only the kind of peace a child experiences. When a baby has eaten and slept well, he is at peace. As for us, we are just older babies whose appearance has slightly changed. When we are in good health, when our bank account is well-stocked and when our professional life is successful, we feel at peace. But this peace is fragile. How can we call this 'peace' when the slightest event poses a threat to it? Everything that exists on this Earth is relative and precarious. But we can rejoin the eternal absolute because God has opened the way for us; we simply have to grasp the rope that He has extended to us.

And yet, there are people who are very detached, very luminous, who have found inner peace and who are not shaken by anything . . .

Are you certain about that?

Isn't the total happiness found in the world of perfect beings a selfish happiness?

Do you know any being that does not have an ego? Attracting benefit is a creational element of the ego: it is an indispensable instrument for motivating us to go towards our perfection. Yet, to cross the border that separates us from the world of perfect beings, we have to purify ourselves of all selfishness. When one reaches perfection, selfishness no longer has any meaning.

Can we say that the prophets were selfish?

They found their salvation in God's satisfaction. They considered themselves to be servants of God, and everything that He commanded them to do, they did in order to satisfy Him, to draw closer to Him and to find a higher happiness.

You have said that the species were directly created in their present form; on the other hand, however, you mentioned the fact that the human nervous system has evolved.

It is an evolution that occurred within one of the species which subsequently did not lose the original form it was created under.

It seems to me that you are upholding a doctrine of reincarnation. Is this correct?

There are numerous reincarnationist theories, such as transmigration or metempsychosis. I have personally found the answers to my questions in the system of 'ascending successive lives'.

What is this system of ascending successive lives?

All human beings have an origin and a purpose, as well as a path that leads to the achievement of that purpose. To cover this path, they are entitled to the same amount of time and the same number of lives. The path can be covered in a single earthly life or it may require numerous lives. Sometimes, there are people who do not reach the goal within the allotted time.

The general and normal direction of this journey is ascendant, going from the inferior to the superior. Thus, a human being cannot regress to the stage of an animal, except in very special cases where a person deviates and commits actions that are so vile he is 'imprisoned' within an animal, or an even lower creature. The period of time during which he is linked to this animal is not deducted from his allotted time, and, like a prisoner who is freed after serving his sentence, he resumes his normal journey after having expiated his deeds.

Why is it necessary to have several lives?

Because almost no human being can make the journey in a single life.

But then, why not a longer life?

One of the reasons is that a person who makes an error and deviates is often trapped in that deviation until the end of his life; a new life presents an opportunity for him to atone for his past and to continue in the right direction.

How can we come to know our primordial cause?

Knowledge of our primordial cause implies several stages. In the first stage, one tries to listen and to believe. In the second stage, one feels and follows. In the third stage, one sees and knows. In the fourth stage, one unites with the Source.

[1] PP, chap VI.

[2] AH 1, p. 333.

[3] A *principle* is an axiom or a fundamental proposition from which other propositions can be derived. *Necessary* means that without which something cannot happen. For example, under normal conditions, a temperature of 100 degrees centigrade is necessary for water to boil.

[4] Borhân ol-Haqq, p. 332.

[5] AH 2, p. 15.

[6] From the Latin *existere*, which means 'to be born from', 'to come out of'.

[7] From 'essence'.

[8] AH 1, p. 335.

[9] AH 1, pp. 334–335.

[10] What is meant here by 'abstract' is that which is beyond physical perception.

[11] Here, we are only concerned with those beings on Earth.

[12] AH 1, p. 312.

[13] AH 1, pp. 333, 319, 311.

[14] AH 1, p. 329.

[15] AH 1, p. 309.

[16] AH 1, p. 329.

[17] AH 1, p. 308.

[18] Traditional saying (*hadith*) attributed to the prophet Mohammad.

[19] AH 1, p. 312.

Study 5

Analogy between the Physical Dimension and the Metaphysical Dimension of Man

---

Introduction. Basic Biological Concepts. The Cell; Cellular Exchanges; Embryology. **Conclusion.**

Introduction

Before beginning this fifth study, which is the first of a series of four devoted to the subject of human beings, I would like to explain why I have chosen to present the metaphysical dimension of man through an analogy to his physical dimension, borrowing terminology from biology and medicine for this purpose. At first, this analogy may seem disconcerting, especially in light of the fact that until now, it has never been made use of by divine persons. To present spiritual truths in a concrete and tangible manner, divine persons have resorted to images adapted to the mentality and culture of their times; hence, the images used by the people of past centuries are no longer suited to modern human beings. Today, a divine person would not say, 'In the other world you shall reap what you have sown in this world'; rather, he would say, 'Study and practise here if you do not want to be unemployed, homeless and an outcast of the spiritual society in the other world.'

To be understood by modern people, spirituality must borrow its images from modern life, especially science, which pervades today's world. One should not infer, however, that in the past spirituality was any less scientific than it is today. It was the same spirituality, but the people of those times did not have the scientific knowledge that is almost commonplace today, and science itself was only in its infancy. In reality, spirituality is so scientific and rigorous that it becomes easy to draw a parallel between our physical dimension and our metaphysical dimension.

A careful study of nature and our environment reveals that creation is based on a few simple recurrent models which combine in various ways. These models govern both the physical and the metaphysical worlds, the models of the physical world being designed after the metaphysical ones. That is why, if we observe and carefully study what is within the reach of our physical senses, it is possible, by analogy, to imagine, deduce, study and more fully understand things which do not fall within the limited scope of our physical senses. It is therefore necessary to begin with models of our physical dimension in order to be able to imagine those of our metaphysical dimension and of the universe at large.

Man is really a microcosm reflecting the macrocosm, and those who study and penetrate the functionings of the human body with a spiritual view can progress more rapidly not only in their scientific research, but in their spiritual research as well. Therefore, we shall approach the human spirit by drawing an analogy between our physical and spiritual dimensions. This study will be devoted to a review of some elementary concepts concerning the cell, cellular exchanges and human embryology as presented by present day science. These concepts will be taken up again in future studies, but it seemed preferable to review them at this point so as to have a clear overview of the matter.[1]

Basic Biological Concepts

Let us first see what a cell is (Fig. 6).

The cell, the elementary unit of all organisms, is a viscous micro-corpuscle with an average length of a few dozen microns – one micron being one thousandth of a millimetre. There are unicellular organisms made up of a single cell (such as an amoeba) and multicellular organisms such as human beings, who comprised 100 to 200 billion cells.

The cell is full of a liquid, rich in proteins, called the cytoplasm, and it is wrapped in a cellular membrane. At the centre of the cell is the nucleus, which also contains a liquid, rich in proteins. The nucleus contains a certain number of filaments called chromosomes.[2] In the chromosomes are the genes invested with hereditary traits. The number of chromosomes for each species is constant; for human beings, this number is 46 (23 pairs). Most of the information the cell will need during its lifetime is gathered inside the nucleus.

The cell is bathed in a surrounding liquid called the extracellular fluid. In order to feed and to reconstitute itself, as well as to reproduce and grow, the cell must draw inorganic salts and organic molecules from this environment. These molecules act as materials for reconstitution and as a source of energy. A certain category of cells, however, draw the necessary energy for their reconstitution from light through cytoplasmic organelles containing pigments (a variety of chlorophyll); this complex mechanism is called photosynthesis.

Similar to the organs of a complex body, a cell possesses numerous elements that fulfil specific functions, which is

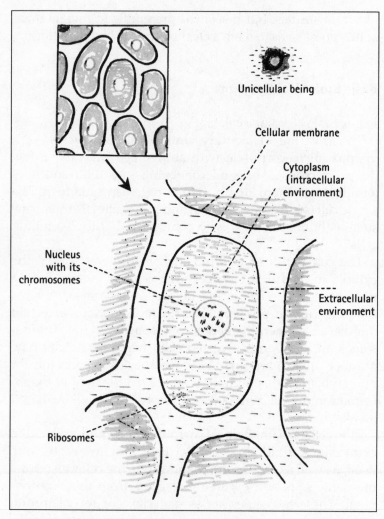

Figure 6   The cell

why we call these elements cellular organelles. For
example, the cellular membrane is a cytoplasmic organelle
that controls the exchanges between the cell and the
extracellular fluid.[3]

On the basis of these few elementary concepts one can already observe, as mentioned before, that creation is founded on a small number of simple models. In fact, there is a striking analogy between the cell, which is the smallest unit of the human body, and the body itself. The organic molecules that the cell draws from the extracellular fluid are to the cell what nourishment is to the human body: material for reconstitution and a source of energy. In addition, we have seen that the cell's nucleus is its information centre: it receives messages and gives orders, just as the brain does in relation to the body. Finally, the cell is made up of organelles that play the same role in the cell as organs do in the body. In the same way, these models can be transposed to the whole universe, and as we shall see, to our metaphysical dimension as well.

Let us now move on to the other basic concept known as osmoregulation (Fig. 7).

For the cell to fulfil all of its functions, it must carry out exchanges with its environment. These exchanges, which take place through the cellular membrane, are, for the most part, subject to the mechanism of osmoregulation.

The two fluids, intra- and extracellular, consist of water in which mineral and organic substances have dissolved. Most of the mineral substances are sodium ions (Na^+) and chloride ions (Cl^-). These substances act in water as gas molecules act in a gaseous atmosphere: they exert pressure on the cellular membrane. This pressure is called osmotic pressure. Osmoregulation involves the set of mechanisms by which living organisms, through exchanges with their environment, control their internal osmotic pressure.

The following experiments help us to better understand the mechanism of osmoregulation. For these experiments, a container is divided into two compartments by a membrane, and two salted solutions are prepared with different concentrations of sodium chloride. For example, one has a concentration of 1 per cent, the other 10 per cent.

In the first experiment, a semi-permeable[4] membrane is placed between the two compartments. One compartment is filled with the more concentrated solution, the other with the less concentrated solution. After a certain period of time, we notice that water passes through the semi-permeable membrane from the less concentrated solution towards the more concentrated solution, so that the two solutions eventually reach equal concentrations. This transfer of water occurs in a passive way as a result of osmotic pressure.

Here, we can make the following observation: apparently, the molecules of water pass through the membrane from the less concentrated solution to the more concentrated solution without any consumption of energy and without any effort on the part of the membrane. Movement, however, implies energy; there must be a force that creates movement. But what is this force that is responsible for the movement of the molecules? We are led to the idea that behind bodies there may be something immaterial, a 'spirit' that confers their effect upon them, or what is called their property. Thus, we could say that what makes molecules of water pass through the semi-permeable membrane is a spirit which we call the 'vegetal spirit'.

In the second experiment, we repeat the same procedure, but with a permeable membrane.[5] This time, the exchanges occur in both directions, meaning that in addition to the passage of water, we also notice that the molecules of sodium chloride move in the opposite direction, from the more concentrated solution to the less concentrated solution. This, too, is a passive exchange which occurs through the mechanism of osmotic pressure. This bi-directional exchange continues until the concentration of the solutions is balanced on both sides of the membrane.

Now, let us see what happens at the level of a biological membrane, for example, a cellular membrane. The cellular

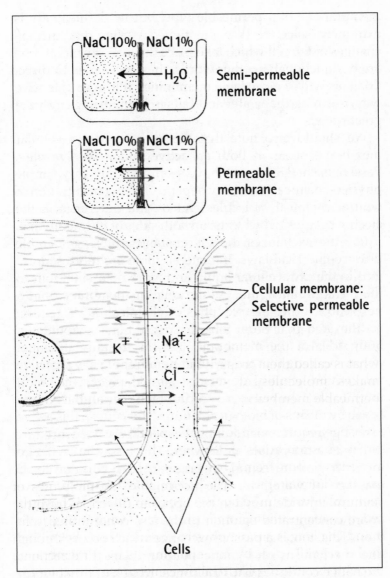

Figure 7   Osmoregulation

membrane is of a permeable type, but its permeability is extremely selective. We mentioned earlier that the exchanges of the cell which take place through the membrane are bi-directional; in other words, they occur in both directions (as with a permeable membrane), but in an intensive way, meaning that water and salts in living beings move at great speeds.

We should also note that the exchanges in a cellular membrane occur in both an active and a passive way. Passive exchanges, as we have seen, abide by very simple physico-chemical laws: they depend on the concentration of neutral chemical molecules and on the difference in the electric charges[6] which exist on both sides of the membrane.

In active exchanges, the cell constantly challenges simple physico-chemical laws. In general, there are more sodium ions in the extracellular liquid and more potassium ions in the intracellular liquid. As the cellular membrane is of a permeable type, simple physico-chemical laws require sodium and potassium ions to exist in equal amounts on both sides of the membrane. Yet this balance does not occur, meaning that the cellular membrane plays an active role which actually dominates simple physico-chemical laws. In fact, the cell expels sodium ions through its membrane by means of biological 'pumps'. Of course, this active exchange requires an additional expenditure of energy.

The question arises as to where this active interference and energy come from. They originate from what we could call the 'animal spirit', which dominates simple physico-chemical laws induced by the vegetal spirit. This is how the cell, the smallest living organism, knows what is useful for it and challenges simple physico-chemical laws belonging to the vegetal spirit by commanding its own membrane, through its animal spirit, to allow penetration of that which is useful and to expel that which is harmful. Some unicellular organisms in nature live in isolation and yet maintain this equilibrium without committing the smallest error.

If we contemplate the cell, we realize that it is well programmed and that everything it has to do is pre-determined. When we consider the spiritual organism of the human being, we shall see that only a part of it – namely, the basharic soul – is programmed like the cell. The angelic soul, however, must itself control the exchanges that occur between the animal elements and the spiritual elements because of the divine spark it carries.

Let us now discuss the last topic: human embryology (Fig. 8). The physical and mental development of a human being begins with fertilization. Fertilization is the process through which the male gamete[7] and the female gamete[8] unite in order to produce a new unicellular organism called a zygote. In the human body, we can distinguish between the so-called somatic cells and the germinal cells which guarantee reproduction. The somatic cells contain 46 chromosomes that are arranged by pairs, each pair consisting of one chromosome from the mother and one from the father. Among these 23 pairs of chromosomes, there are 22 pairs of autosomes (non-sex chromosomes) and one pair of sex chromosomes – XY (for men) or XX (for women).

The primordial germinal cells,[9] which also have 46 chromosomes, divide and reduce the number of their chromosomes by half in order to give birth to adult germinal cells (gametes) that are ready for fertilization. The reduction of the number of chromosomes by half is required so that the fusion of the male gamete and the female gamete does not produce a child with twice the number of chromosomes of his parents (in which case it would be a non-viable monster). Each male or female gamete carries 22 non-sex chromosomes, as well as an X sex chromosome for the female gamete and an X or Y chromosome for the male gamete. It sometimes happens that in the course of the gametes' formation, anomalies occur in the number of chromosomes. For example, one

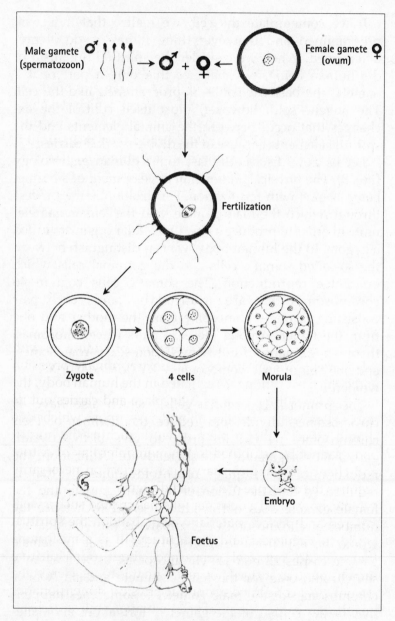

Figure 8   Human embryology

chromosome may be lacking or there may be one chromosome too many; in such cases, the child is born with 45 or 47 chromosomes. This phenomenon is one of the sources of congenital anomalies.

The fusion of the female and the male gametes produces a new cell, the zygote (46 chromosomes), which develops in the following way: it divides itself in two and produces two cells; then it divides in 4, in 8, and then in 16, until it becomes like a small mulberry called a morula. The first eight weeks of the intra-uterine life of the child constitute the embryonic period; during this time, the child is most vulnerable and congenital malformations may occur. Beyond the eighth week and until the actual birth, one speaks of the foetal period.

Conclusion

This study of a few basic biological concepts should not be considered as just a brief presentation providing us with the elements for an analogy. The extraordinary precision with which everything is regulated in the human body, the fact that everything is in its right place and carries out its duties flawlessly, implies the idea – upon which one should reflect – that a piece of work such as the human body cannot be attributed to the mere interplay of nature and chance. On the contrary, such perfection necessarily requires the existence of a perfect designer.

Now, how could a designer who has created such a well-ordered and perfect material world abandon the spiritual world to vagueness and inexactitude? It is a misfortune that we do not feel concerned about our spiritual dimension, that it does not really matter to us. Generally, we only feel concerned about our physical dimension: our health, our career, our financial situation, our search for pleasure. But we are unconscious of our soul's health, of our spiritual destiny and of our eternal condition. The essential aim of the analogy between our physical dimension and our metaphysical dimension, which we will elaborate further in future studies, is precisely to awaken us and to make us understand how important it is to take these matters seriously. We will not escape physical death, and keeping our eyes shut will not lead us anywhere.

People today have a tendency not to believe in the existence of another dimension because they have only conducted intellectual or individual research on this topic. Yet they devote a substantial amount of time and effort to know their physical dimension even better and to ensure their physical well-being. If only one-tenth of all those efforts were directed towards their metaphysical dimension, they would make discoveries which would radically alter their outlook.

We actually lack true spiritual scientists, capable of conducting research, beginning, for example, by specifying the common points found in numerous spiritual experiences. However, just as every individual has the potential capacity to become a scientist in the material domain, every individual also has the possibility of becoming a spiritual scientist. The condition for doing so is to adopt the same rational approach as that of true spiritual scientists, beginning by studying and practising spirituality with the seriousness and mindset of a student, in the same way that one would study and practise any other concrete, exact and experimental science.

Questions

Is there any particular reason why God has based all creation on a series of simple and repetitive models, or is it simply for us to understand better?

Perfection is in simplicity and justice.

What you say regarding the vegetal spirit and the animal spirit seems totally arbitrary: one could just as well say that this energy comes from something else which scientists have yet to discover.

Some scientists also believe that there is something beyond matter. Ostad Elahi named this something 'spirit' or 'soul', and he made distinctions between various categories of spirits, such as mineral, vegetal and animal spirits.

But why is it that water, which is not vegetal, is animated by a vegetal spirit, as seen in the mechanism of osmoregulation?

The spirits or souls which come from the Earth (and not from the spiritual world) – namely, the spirits found from mineral to bashar (human being without an angelic soul) – form a continuous strand, and at each stage (mineral, vegetal, animal and basharic) one finds traces of the preceding stages. For example, the animal spirit bears within itself mineral and vegetal spirits, and the mineral spirit already contains a hint of what the vegetal spirit will be.

What exactly do you mean by 'spiritual scientist'? Is that a mystic or a theologian?

God has given us four pillars which we must rely upon to perfect ourselves: the soul, the body, the spiritual world and the material world. A spiritual scientist is someone who knows and perfectly respects the balance between the rights of these four pillars and the duties which pertain to each of them. A mystic is someone who wants to travel on the path of perfection solely with love and illumination, neglecting the body and the material world. A theologian is someone who relies solely on his intellect, or in other words on his body, and neglects the other three pillars.

One could summarize things in the following way:

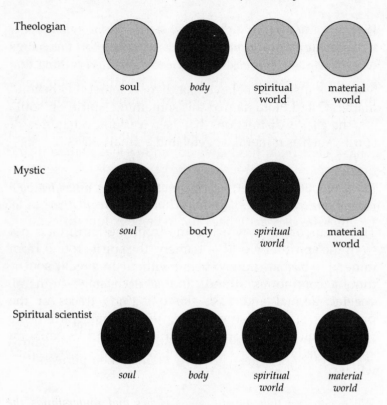

You are linking the intellect to the body, but isn't the intellect an emanation of the angelic soul? Animals do not have an intellect.

The intellect is an animal intelligence which contains the ferment of the angelic soul; however, the origin of the intellect is still the brain, and therefore the body.

You have said that spirituality is not accessible to our physical senses. Under these conditions, then, how can we set out to conduct research, and with what means and devices can we do so? What knowledge should we rely upon?

As is the case with any science, there have always been researchers and scientists in spirituality who have left us a heritage, and whose successors have taken over from where they left off. For example, the authentic prophets and saints were spiritual scientists. If we could gather everything that remains from their lives, their actions and their sayings, and if we could filter all of this so as to eliminate the impurities which have been mixed with them over the course of time, we would have a reliable basis to rest upon. This, in fact, is what Ostad Elahi has achieved, and he has named it 'the quintessence of religions'. On the basis of this knowledge, it is within ourselves that we must find the means to carry out our research. In every human being, there are potential faculties he can actualize that will help him to conduct research and distinguish between right and wrong.

You have said that we all have the capacity to become spiritual scientists. Does that mean that we can become prophets?

There is only a difference of mission, and not of level, between divine persons (authentic prophets and saints) and ordinary persons who have attained their perfection.

When you say that anyone who studies and understands the functioning of the human body with a spiritual view can make spiritual discoveries, what exactly do you mean by 'spiritual viewpoint'? By asking this, I have in mind the example of Pasteur, who was both a scientist and a man of faith, yet he did not make any spiritual discoveries.

How can you be so sure?

In your opinion, why don't people conduct research in spirituality as they would do in medicine, for example?

Human beings always turn their attention to what they perceive to be tangible, things that are apparent to their physical senses, while they have a tendency to neglect, and even completely ignore, anything that is not present in the sphere of their physical senses. As long as their physical well-being is at stake, human beings try to deepen their knowledge, but when it comes to spirituality their reflection becomes superficial. Humans have penetrated the most remote levels of matter, yet they are content with staying at the surface of spirituality because, on the rare occasions when they have tried to increase their knowledge of spiritual matters, they were unable to find convincing answers to their questions. As a result, human beings no longer believe in spirituality, and since they do not believe in it, they have stopped searching.

You are presenting spirituality as a kind of medical science of the soul, so I would like to know what place psychology holds in your system of thought?

I have a great deal of respect for psychologists, psychiatrists and psychoanalysts, and it often happens that we collaborate in the medical domain. Unfortunately, traditional psychology and psychoanalysis were originally founded on a view of the human psyche that denies the soul. Now if it is true that one can develop an understanding of the psyche with such sciences, and if it is true that one can also reach a certain level in the observation of facts and symptoms, it nevertheless remains impossible to reach any precise and exact etiology of these facts and symptoms without taking the soul into account. If psychology considered this element, it could become a complete science; spirituality and psychology would then follow the same line, because the aim of spirituality is to know oneself in order to know God, and self-knowledge begins with the study of the psyche.

You have talked several times about the importance of studying and practising spirituality with the seriousness and mindset of a student. Can you elaborate on this point?

One has to consider spirituality as an experimental science in the full sense of the term, and like any other science, one has to approach it with the mindset and seriousness of a student. Spirituality is not the search for pseudo-spiritual amusements such as levitation or reading people's thoughts. Spirituality can be compared to medicine: to become a physician of the soul (in other words, to become perfect), a person has to learn the physiology, pathology, anatomy and immune system of the soul, as well as the traps that await it, the pathogenic agents which seek to attack it, etc. This information is difficult to attain and requires painstaking effort.

You said that spirituality is scientific, but how is it possible to analyse faith in a scientific way?

Faith is an attraction towards Transcendence. It comes from the gravitational force that the divine entity exerts upon us, and this attraction manifests itself through a particular feeling which we call faith. The closer we draw to God the more our faith grows, because the closer we come to a pole of attraction, the stronger that attraction becomes. On the other hand, the worse our behaviour is, the more 'rusted' we are, the less attracted we are and the less faith we have. And when I speak of faith here, I mean sincere and pure faith.

In general, your view of spirituality is not very encouraging. It seems that everything comes down to formulas, as if everything can be summed up by rights and duties.

But that's how it really is. The concept of studying at a university is no more encouraging – it is the aim which must motivate us. As soon as we talk of spirituality, people immediately think of obtaining quick spiritual pleasures, but this view is erroneous. It comes from the heritage of the mystics and it pervades our culture, making us associate visions and supernatural powers with spirituality. All these things are just spiritual amusements which cannot lead us to the goal. What does lead us to the goal is studying and practising with the mindset of a student. And like academic studies, the path of perfection has its own bonuses, bringing about effects such as serenity and light.

Ostad Elahi has mentioned a number of these effects, mainly in the following passage:

> The result of life in this world can be summarized in six points: nostalgia (all good things must pass – youth, happiness, joy – and when everything has passed, nothing remains but nostalgia); envy (we do not get what we desire so we become envious and say to ourselves, 'This person obtained such and such, but I did not . . .'); regret ('Why didn't I do this or that in order to obtain this other thing?'); remorse (all our deeds contrary to ethics and humanity are always on our minds, and we reproach ourselves for them); bitter memories (all our failures, all the injustices we have been subjected to without being able to avenge ourselves, etc.); and finally, fear of death (this is the worst of all: we live in perpetual anguish, always wondering when the time will come).
>
> Every human being is confronted with these six phenomena, but someone who directs his efforts towards spirituality neutralizes their effects. To the extent that he has always been involved in spirituality, the discomforts of life and bitter memories do not affect him; envy does not even cross his mind; he does not have any reason to feel remorse; he has no regrets or feelings of nostalgia, and he does not fear death. As long as he lives in this world, he is serene and satisfied, and the same is true when he leaves for the other world.[11]

---

[1] Since these studies are meant for the general public, the scientific concepts have been simplified and presented in a schematic way.

[2] Each of them is formed by a double strand of DNA (deoxyribonucleic acid) molecules, carrying various genes.

³ Another example of organelles is the numerous granules of ribosomes (more than 10,000 in each cell): they are also considered as cytoplasmic organelles and they play a major role in the synthesis of polypeptide chains of proteins. There are, of course, many other kinds of organelles.

⁴ Semi-permeable: allows only water to pass through.

⁵ Permeable: allows water and certain dissolved substances to pass through.

⁶ In a chemical solution, for example salt water, a certain number of neutral molecules, such as sodium chloride (NaCl) in this case, dissolve and transform themselves into ionized atoms of Na^+ and Cl^-, providing the solution with its specific electric charge.

⁷ Spermatozoon or male germinal cell.

⁸ Ovum or female germinal cell.

⁹ Located in the genital glands.

¹⁰ AH 1, p. 620

Study 6

The Spiritual Gametes

Introduction

The Creator is unique, necessarily perfect, absolute and the very source of reason. Among His numerous attributes, it is by His grace, His generosity and His justice that He has created creatures so that they may benefit from His grace. The created being, however, is necessarily imperfect, for it would be absurd to think that the Creator, who is perfect, would create something equal to Himself. Being imperfect, the created being is also incomplete, for if it were otherwise, it would be unique and independent.

To benefit fully from divine grace, the created being must become completely conscious, which is to say that it must perfect itself to the point of reaching total concrete consciousness. To reach that point, however, it must first complete itself. Hence, creatures are created in complementary pairs so that each can combine with its counterpart; this is the essential condition for developing the potential to evolve towards one's perfection (Fig. 9).

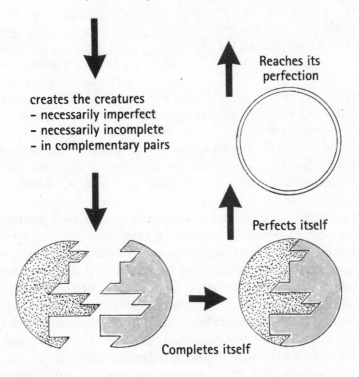

Figure 9 The origin and aim of creatures

A being attains perfection when its essential reality, having covered the very long and hazardous course of the causal worlds, eventually reaches the metacausal world, at the end of the process of spiritual perfection. It then frees itself from the realm of the relative and enters the domain of the absolute;[1] it reaches its own perfection and then is called a 'perfect being'. But, to acquire the potential to fulfil its functions and to evolve towards its perfection, each creature must necessarily combine with its own counterpart.

There are two kinds of counterparts: material and spiritual. Material counterparts are those which combine together to generate a new being, in the same way that oxygen and nitrogen combine to form air. The male and female gametes are also an example of material counterparts. As we saw in the previous lecture, the human body is formed by the union of two cells: the female gamete and the male gamete. Both are creatures in the full sense of the term, and both complement one another. Their union produces a new unicellular organism, a zygote, capable of developing and producing a human being.

It is precisely by drawing an analogy with human embryology that we can better understand how the two spiritual counterparts (the angelic soul and the basharic soul) combine to form the 'self'. It is indeed possible to compare our angelic soul to a celestial gamete, or a positive pole, and our basharic soul to a terrestrial gamete, or a negative pole. Something is lacking in each of these two spiritual gametes which is to be found in the other. One could say that each of them only has half the chromosomes of a complete spiritual cell. Their union forms a complete whole, which we may call the spiritual zygote or the 'self'.

This spiritual zygote will then produce a spiritual child, which by itself will have to regulate (this is a very important point) its own growth and development, because unlike the body, the growth and development of the soul is not automatic. 'Self-regulated' growth is the process of going through the different stages of the soul – childhood (immaturity), adolescence and maturity – under the direction of one's own judgment and will. We do not mention old age here, since there is no old age for the soul; the soul does not age. Maturity means perfection, and it does not entail ageing.

We are therefore responsible for this process of growth and development because our free-will, although relative, is nonetheless determining. In this regard, the self-regulated growth of the soul, which cannot occur without the contribution of the body, does not begin until the body reaches the age of responsibility. To avoid any confusion, it should also be noted that the various ages of the human soul do not correspond in any systematic way to physical age: one can have a mature soul in the body of a child, or a young soul in the body of a mature person.

Let us now examine the characteristics of these two spiritual gametes, the angelic soul and the basharic soul, which combine so that we can develop ourselves and grow.

The Celestial Gamete or Angelic Soul

The celestial gamete, or angelic soul, is that part of the human being which comes directly from one of the three spiritual spaces.[2] It is formed of two essential constituents: the divine spark and reason (Fig. 10).[3]

The Divine Spark

The divine spark is also called the 'divine breath'. Although it is not the soul of God, it comes directly from God. Since no one will ever come to know what the divine essence is made of, one cannot say what the divine spark is made of. In principle, every human being endowed with an angelic soul carries the divine spark, but sometimes, when the faults of a person exceed certain limits, he loses his divine spark. The divine spark automatically separates itself from him in the same way that a magnet separates itself from rusted iron; his soul then loses its brightness, its life, its transparency, and he finds himself alone facing his faults, tarnished, like a wreck.

Reason

Reason consists of transcendent reason and executive reason.

Transcendent Reason
Transcendent reason is the centre of all information and all conscious decisions of human beings. It is the eternal centre of total concrete consciousness. What is total concrete consciousness (Fig. 11)? Every being that comes out of nothingness and into existence has a certain perception of itself; this is also true about minerals and plants. Every being has an intimate and immediate sensation of its own existence and state. The essential reality of a being comes down to its consciousness. What are we, essentially? We are nothing but consciousness. Flesh, bones, neurons, skin, blood – all these things are just instruments. What are we right now? Me, this 'I', who is speaking to you at this very moment, is consciousness and nothing else; and you, listening to me, you are consciousness in the act of listening. The more a being perfects itself, the more its consciousness deepens and expands, that is, in addition to mere superficial self-perception, the consciousness begins to perceive its inner states, and the more it perceives its inner reality, the more its external perception expands. Thus, its knowledge

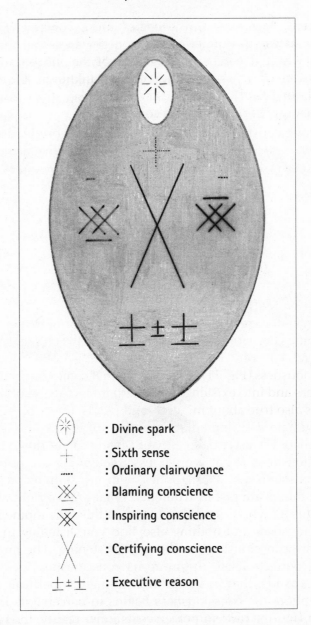

Figure 10   Representation of the components of the angelic soul

deepens, increases and becomes more concrete. Ostad Elahi states: 'In human beings, consciousness can reach a level where it perceives the reality of the entire universe with such clarity that nothing remains unknown. It is at the level of total concrete consciousness that human consciousness rejoins divine consciousness.'

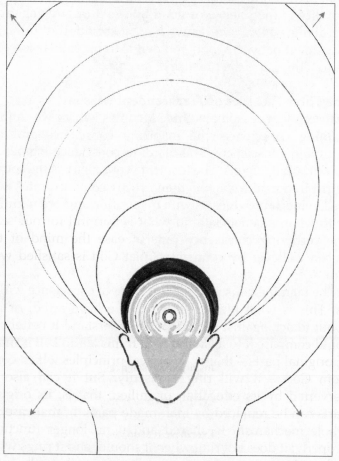

Figure 11   Total concrete consciousness. 'The more one perceives one's inner reality, the more one's external perception expands'

Thus, transcendent reason is the eternal centre of total concrete consciousness. It is the centre of understanding the real truth of every thing; of distinguishing between good and evil, usefulness and harm. It is the centre of free will, conscious or transcendent will, conscious intelligence, of rational thought, transcendent creativity, eternal memory, etc. All these qualities belong to the angelic soul alone. Ethics and morals also belong to the angelic soul, for morality is the science of good and evil originating from the divine source, and as we have just said, the source of judgement between good and evil is transcendent reason.[4] As for ethics, it is the practice of morals.

The Three Faculties of Transcendent Reason
Transcendent reason has three faculties, which we call the blaming conscience, the inspiring conscience and the certifying conscience. 'The blaming conscience blames us for our wrong deeds. The inspiring conscience is the source of inspiration, the channel that directly communicates with the Divine; it provides us with inspiration and premonition as to what is beneficial and what is harmful for our soul. The certifying conscience puts at ease the mind of the sincere believer by confirming that God is satisfied with him.'[5]

The blaming conscience is the voice of conscience within us. This is what blames us when we have acted, or are about to act, against morality. To understand it better, we could compare it to an alarm bell. If this alarm bell is made of original parts – that is, of ethical principles which come from God – it will ring advisedly. But it can also be perverted by its education or milieu; that is, its original parts can be replaced by man-made parts. In that case, its whole mechanism is altered and it no longer functions properly: it does not ring when it should, and it rings when it should not. For example, in a tribe of cannibals, the act of eating human flesh does not set off the alarm, which has been put out of order by the cultural milieu. In the same way, one might say that the blaming conscience of a killer is out of order.

The blaming conscience also engenders a sense of guilt. The excess or the lack of that sense of guilt, whether justified or not, are equally pathological, and the remedy for them is to receive a proper and rational spiritual education, an education that comes from the Divine Source.

The inspiring conscience, when it is not faltering, inspires us with what is good or right and what is evil or wrong; in other words, it inspires us as to whether something is in accordance with the Divine or not. It comes into play whenever we ask ourselves whether an action is right or wrong. Also, the inspiring conscience allows us to perceive the reality behind commonly held opinions or instinctively detect a spiritual charlatan. If it is not rusted or subject to interferences, it communicates with the Source and brings us an answer.

As for the certifying conscience, it creates within us the certitude that we have been acting in accordance with divine satisfaction. It manifests itself through a feeling of deep and reassuring joy, which is inexplicable in material terms. This feeling is also referred to as having a 'good conscience'.

These three faculties are thus the instruments of our transcendent reason, and it is essential for the soul's perfection to use them judiciously.

Executive Reason

The other aspect of reason is the executive reason. As its name indicates, the executive reason is in charge of executing the commands of the transcendent reason, and it determines the means through which to do so. For example, if the transcendent reason orders the executive reason to help someone in need, it is up to the executive reason to determine the means for doing so. When the executive reason manages to control the faculties of the basharic soul,[6] those faculties become its instruments.

Celestial Reason

The aim of the growth and development of the angelic soul is to perfect the 'self' by developing our transcendent reason, which must reach the stage of celestial reason. Celestial reason is that which knows how to maintain a perfect equilibrium between the requirements of our material life and those of our spiritual life, that is, between the four pillars of our existence: this world, the next world, our soul and our body. The divine spark is the leaven or essence of celestial reason, but for it to develop and actualize, it must be fuelled by the actions of the executive reason.

The Characteristic Ingredients of the Angelic Soul

The constituent substance or the 'solvent' of the angelic soul is dignity tinged with divine love. When we go to the other world, what dominates our entire being is a sense of our own dignity, along with a very powerful sensation of divine love. This dignity spontaneously expresses itself as soon as we enter the other world, just as pride spontaneously expresses itself as long as we live in this world. Indeed, here the prevailing characteristics belong to the basharic soul, whereas in the other world the predominant characteristics are those of the angelic soul. With such an intense feeling of self-dignity, one can imagine, then, what the soul experiences when it has been committing undignified acts during its earthly life: a terrible feeling of shame and humiliation, accompanied by the torment of not being able to approach the Beloved.

The characteristic ingredients of the angelic soul are rectitude, sincerity, love of honour and glory, as well as naiveté, excessiveness, ignorance, an attraction for spiritual pleasures, etc. It must also be noted that, in its pure state, it does not have any of the characteristic ingredients of the terrestrial gamete, such as pride, sensuality, anger, cunning, animosity, etc. The grandeur, the brilliance and the power of the angelic soul depend upon its capacity. The angelic soul is constantly in motion, but prior to combining for the first time with its counterpart, the terrestrial gamete, it lacks any precise shape or concrete consciousness, and it is not free to leave its original space.

The Sixth Sense and Ordinary Clairvoyance

According to the explanations given by Ostad Elahi, the sixth sense is a faculty of the soul which enables one to see God, to travel through time and space, to read the inner thoughts of others, etc. The sixth sense is different from the spiritual senses: its awakening is a divine gift, whereas the awakening of the spiritual senses is related to one's degree of perfection and requires consistent effort and self-education. God alone can awaken the sixth sense, either totally or partially, for our whole life or for a certain period of time. Also, the sixth sense works without any preliminary preparation or specific techniques such as asceticism or meditation. When it is awakened, its use depends upon our will. However, God only awakens the sixth sense in those whom He knows will not use it for personal profit.

Ordinary clairvoyance is a faculty which is inherently present in some people, independent of their faith, spiritual level or will. It enables them to see and even to foretell some common things in a more or less clear and exact way, as is the case, for example, with clairvoyant people.

The Terrestrial Gamete or Basharic Soul

Let us now describe the terrestrial gamete, or basharic soul, which is the necessary counterpart of the celestial gamete. Why speak of a 'terrestrial' gamete? Because the basharic soul originates from the earth and is the end result of the process of perfection of mineral, vegetal and animal souls.[7] Its characteristic ingredients therefore include mineral and vegetal properties, as well as the characteristics of all animals. The solvent of the basharic soul is pride tinged with terrestrial love. In addition to being a counterpart, the basharic soul can also be considered a receptacle for the angelic soul. It consists of two components: the worker self and the imperious self (Fig. 12).

The Worker Self

The worker self is the instinctive and peaceful force which makes all the organs function together and ensures the preservation of life. For example, control of the automatic vegetative processes of our body is one of its functions (ie, the growth of hair, nails, etc).

The Imperious Self

The imperious self is an internal, hyper-active reasoning power which, when uncontrolled, brings us to do evil. The imperious self is the manifestation of destructive, ferocious and predatory animal characteristics that are in dis-equilibrium. It is rebellious, stubborn and intrusive. As Ostad Elahi said: *'It is comparable to a dormant demon in every human being.'*
The imperious self manifests itself through the imbalance of various faculties of the basharic soul, mainly the

Figure 12   The worker self and the imperious self

irascible faculty, the concupiscent faculty and the imaginative faculty. It should be noted that the imperious self is not a real entity or a creation *per se*, but rather only an aspect or mode of the basharic soul; in other words, the imperious self has a functional existence and not a substantial one, for it originates from the malfunctioning of our animal instincts and only exists through the excess or lack of the three faculties mentioned above. It is the collective or individual imbalance of these faculties that generates this driving force known as the imperious self.

The imperious self is not a creation as such, because God never creates anything evil.

The Faculties of the Basharic Soul

The irascible faculty is the faculty of anger. When it is not mastered by reason, it engenders predation, aggression, transgression, oppression, etc. However, if the executive reason succeeds, after considerable effort, in dominating this faculty, it will become an asset, as it is the weapon by which the executive reason can bring the other two faculties of concupiscence and imagination to order and thereby restore equilibrium. Besides, without this faculty, human beings would not be able to defend their rights because they would have no courage, no firmness and no sense of honour.

The concupiscent faculty is the faculty of appetence. In excess, it engenders 'stomachic' love, lust and other appetites such as greed, jealousy, the quest for pleasures, etc. When insufficient, it engenders depression, asthenia, a lack of appetence, etc. In equilibrium, it generates decency and restraint.

Unlike our transcendent reason, which has a broad and global view, the imaginative faculty has a scope which is narrow and limited to details and particulars. By nature, it engenders cunning, intrigue, deception, obsessive doubt, fussiness, etc, but when it is under the control of the executive reason, it engenders ingenuity and prudence.

The Creational Factors of the Self

Apart from certain exceptions, the union between the basharic soul and the angelic soul takes place at birth. According to Ostad Elahi, there are seven creational factors which determine the physical, psychological and spiritual capacities of the child. Parents can play a direct and important role in determining the first six factors, and can have a favourable effect on the seventh (Fig. 13).

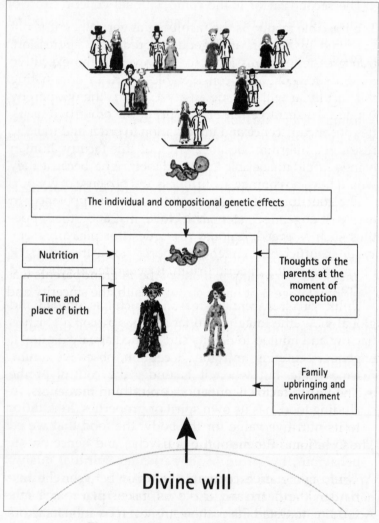

Figure 13   The seven creational factors

- The first factor is the particular genetic effect – that is, the individual genetic effects of the father, the mother, the grandparents and the great-grandparents, amounting to a total of 14 people.

- The second factor is the compositional genetic effect of these 14 ancestors; it is because of this compositional genetic effect that even two identical twins are not completely alike.

- The third factor is the thoughts of the father and mother at the moment of conception. Generally, the thoughts of human beings are recorded inside them as well as outside. At the moment of conception, the receptivity of the gametes increases: the thoughts of the parents are more easily imprinted upon them and in part determine the psyche of the child. For example, if the thoughts of the parents at the moment of conception are pure and sincere, the child will have a natural tendency towards honesty and sincerity. The purity of the parents' intentions also favours the fixing of positive characteristics from the 14 ancestors. For example, if one of the 14 grandparents was more intelligent or had a stronger faith, the sincerity and purity of the parents' intentions will favour the fixing of the corresponding genes. Another outcome of this purity of intention is that it can prevent the transmission of certain genetic diseases to the child.

- The fourth factor is nutrition: everything that exists, including food, has its own spirit or properties. In addition to its nutritive value for the body, the food that we eat also has an influence on our psyche, and hence on our behaviour, by virtue of its particular spiritual quality. Thus, some diets promote sensitivity, while others harden the heart and make us insensitive to the misfortune of others. Just as the spirit of food influences our psyche, we, too, can positively or negatively influence the spirit of the food we eat through our intentions and our actions. For example, the spirit of the food that is acquired by honest means is beneficial to the soul of the person who consumes it. The food involved in the formation of the gametes therefore has an effect, as does the food that is consumed by the mother during pregnancy and breast-feeding, as well as the food eaten by the child from birth onwards.

- The fifth factor is the effect of time and place. The moment of birth and the place of birth, as well as other factors at the time of birth, have a more or less determining influence. For example, it has been observed that the chances of developing schizophrenia are greater among children born in winter.[8]

- The sixth factor is education and the socio-cultural environment. This implies, on the one hand, the education and the socio-cultural environment of the parents, and on the other hand, the education and the socio-cultural environment of the child, from birth to the age of responsibility.

- The seventh factor, which prevails over the other six factors, is the Divine Will. The Divine Will comes into play on the basis of the merits of the soul that is to occupy the body.[9] The Divine Will, then, determines which soul will enter the body according to the six factors previously mentioned, and by the same token, it determines the interplay of those six factors according to the merits of the particular soul intended for that body. It should be noted that the parents' pure and sincere faith plays a very important role in determing the direction of the Divine Will.

It is the ensemble of these factors which causes some children to become remarkable individuals, even geniuses in the material or spiritual domains, and others to be without any particular ability in either domain. These factors are also responsible for the willpower that some children have to succeed in life, to resist harmful temptations and to avoid falling into the trap of drug addiction or delinquency, while others cannot resist negative influences, easily succumb to them and are even predisposed to being marginalized.

These seven factors have a considerable spiritual influence on the formation of the individual, from the moment of conception until about the age of 24, when the period of voluntary psycho-spiritual maturation begins.

Conclusion

If I have insisted so much in the course of this lecture on the details of the constitution and development of the soul, on the analogy of the gametes, it is in order to go against a common tendency that people have to put the soul somewhere 'up above', as some intangible and ethereal entity. One should understand – and I cannot emphasize this enough – that 'natural' spirituality, which will guide us towards the metacausal world and eternity, must be considered as a complete science, an extremely systematic and precise science. Death does not exist, and our eternal abode is elsewhere.

Now, if we are going to live somewhere else we should make preparations, and since nothing is ever given free, we must work for what we want to get; this is a law of creation. The foundation or basis of our spiritual life is the spiritual work that we can accomplish here on earth and nowhere else. If we spend our life in negligence, we lose time and we place our future at risk. Believe me, we must really be concerned with tomorrow. We often have a somewhat superficial view of spirituality: we tend to think that practising spirituality means withdrawing from life and praying in some remote corner of the world. But that is not spirituality. Spiritual life begins when two gametes, terrestrial and celestial, form a spiritual embryo. Well, a laboratory is needed for this responsible being, and that laboratory is nothing other than society.

Questions

You have said that the more our consciousness develops, the more our view expands and the more we are able to understand the whole universe; but how can we understand the whole universe when we are so small and limited?

In the spiritual world, distance and volume are irrelevant. The closer we come to the divine, the more our view expands, because we have managed to penetrate the black layer that we have formed with our imperious self. Every negative thought, action or behaviour produces a thick black smoke which covers the soul and limits its vision. In reality, however, we could say that the soul's vision is unlimited and does not face any obstacles such as matter, time or space. Thus, by trying to purify our thoughts and our intentions, we wash away all these layers which are covering our soul, and when it is completely purified, our vision encompasses the whole universe. The more we delve within ourselves and the more we purify ourselves, the more our vision expands, until it eventually reaches infinity and rejoins God. Then, the whole universe is within the reach of our senses.

What is the role of the divine spark in the angelic soul?

The divine spark is to the angelic soul of human beings what the angelic soul is to the basharic soul and what life is to an animal.

What difference is there between a creature that has that divine spark and a creature that only has an angelic soul without the divine spark?

Does a ten-carat diamond have the same value as ten tons of coal? The divine spark is the spark of the divine essence. Bearing that single spark of the divine essence is what confers a divine value upon a human being.

Sometimes I have an inner dialogue, just as if two selves were arguing within me; does that come from the different elements which make up the self?

Exactly. All the elements of the angelic soul and the basharic soul that constitute the self are active within us and make themselves heard. Ostad Elahi, by the way, has provided an example of the kind of inner dialogue which can occur between the imperious self and the blaming conscience:

> The powerful voice of the imperious self makes itself heard and argues by saying: 'Now really, where is the other world? Who has seen this other world? Who has ever come back to attest it? These are all lies. The only thing that exists is in this world; you should make the most of the short time you have.' The blaming conscience protests and tells us: 'You wretched fool, do not listen to him. Beware and do not let yourself be tricked by the imperious self. God help you if you listen to him.'

According to what you said in your study, the soul also has excessive tendencies which one has to master.

Yes, the soul also experiences excessiveness and imbalance, and it is up to the celestial reason to control it.

What is the exact distinction between pride and dignity?

Pride means the advantageous and overstated opinion that a person holds of his personal value. It derives from ignorance: the proud person does not see his faults and attributes qualities to himself which he does not have, or which do not have any real moral value. Dignity, on the other hand, is inspired in a person who has real and high-level intelligence and moral values, and it is accompanied by an inner modesty. While pride brings about blindness as to oneself, dignity opens the mind as to one's real worth.

Do the two gametes separate after death?

No. The basharic soul annihilates itself in the angelic soul, and its effects continue to live in the angelic soul.

'When the executive reason manages to dominate the faculties of the basharic soul, these faculties become its instruments.' Can you give an example of this?

For example, one way of fighting against a temptation deriving from the concupiscent faculty is to force oneself to become inwardly angry in order to drive away that temptation. In this manner, the executive reason uses the irascible faculty to subjugate the concupiscent faculty.

You have been speaking of the gene of faith. Is faith hereditary?

Parallel to the genetics of the body, there are genetics of the soul which explain why some people are more predisposed to having faith than others. The spiritual heredity of each person comes from his ancestors or from his past lives.

Since it is the irascible faculty which provides us with courage when it is in balance, could we say that the angelic soul is deprived of it?

When it comes to the angelic soul, courage does not have

the same meaning. The courage we have been speaking of consists in overcoming a fear which has a terrestrial, animal origin. But the fear that the soul can experience is the fear of being far from God; this is a fear we should not fight against, for it is extremely positive. The courageous person is one whose angelic soul governs his basharic instincts.

Which faults can cause someone to lose the divine spark?

It depends on the person, the level of the soul, the circumstances, the time, etc. Some crimes may bring about loss of the divine spark, but only God judges which.

Isn't there some injustice in the fact that souls can be more or less lofty, bright, etc?

Do not confuse harmony with injustice. When they reach perfection, creatures are so overwhelmed by happiness that they do not wish to be anything other than what they are. As Ostad Elahi says: 'Their feelings of happiness and well-being share the same quality; however, the higher their rank, the deeper their knowledge of the divine secret.'

You have said that God does not create evil, but everything that exists has been created by God, which would seem to include evil.

Evil is a complication produced by certain creatures who make bad use of their free will. If black smoke comes out of the exhaust of a badly tuned car, the manufacturer is not to blame.

You have referred to the blaming conscience and the certifying conscience. I think I understand the meaning of those two expressions, but I am not sure I can find the inspiring conscience within myself; perhaps it is rusted. How can we feel it, and how can we have it function properly?

To have the inspiring conscience function properly, as well as the other two consciences, one must have a pure and sincere faith in God and must want to apply His principles; anyone that acts in this way will be inspired. When we reflect on a problem and ask ourselves whether what we are doing is right or not, whether God is satisfied with that action or not, an inspiration enters our thoughts. All of us have been inspired, and more than just once in our lives. Those who do not have faith claim that they themselves thought of that which, in reality, was inspired to them.

Can the inspiring conscience mislead us?

Yes. If the inspiring conscience is sound and not subjected to any kind of interference, its inspirations will be correct, but if it is disturbed or if it has degenerated under the influence of some disease of the soul, it gives distorted results.

How can we tell if an inspiration is right or wrong?

If our transcendent reason is healthy, we should use it in accordance with moral and divine principles; if not, one has to ask.

Whom can we ask?

Someone whose transcendent reason is healthy and sound.

But how can we distinguish such a person?

Someone whose transcendent reason is healthy applies the fundamental religious and ethical principles as if they were second nature, without expecting any personal profit in return.

[1] We are only concerned here with what is relative or absolute in relation to the being itself.

[2] Cf. Study 3.

[3] The distinction between the different constituents of the angelic soul and the basharic soul is primarily for didactic purposes. In reality, these components combine and interweave, forming what we call the self; the basharic soul and the angelic soul are united and they form a single entity, even though it is possible to distinguish between the effects coming from the former and those coming from the latter.

[4] By 'good' we mean what the Creator – or a divine source – considers to be good, and by 'evil' we mean what *He* considers to be evil.

[5] AH 1, p. 248.

[6] Cf. infra.

[7] See PP, chaps III and IV.

[8] *Comprehensive Textbook of Psychiatry VI*, vol. 2, Harold I. Kaplan and Benjamin J. Sadock.

[9] By 'body', what is meant here is the physical body plus the psychological potential.

Study 7

The Spiritual Ecosystem

> **Spirits of the Spiritual Ecosphere.** Positive Spirits; Negative Spirits. **The Spiritual Environment.** Abiotic Factors: Radiation, Gravity, the Spiritual Atmosphere, Temperature, Water; Biotic Factors: Relations with Saprophyte and Tempter Spirits, Relations with Venomous Persons, Relations with Divine Persons; Relations with the Face of God. **Conclusion.**

The ecosystem is a whole formed on the one hand by the environment, and on the other, by the organisms which live in it. All of the terrestrial ecosystems together are collectively called the ecosphere. Parallel to the physical ecosystems are the spiritual ecosystems, and all of these spiritual ecosystems form yet another ecosystem, the spiritual ecosphere. This spiritual ecosphere consists of the spiritual environment (the spiritual atmosphere, light, etc) as well as all the beings that live in it, which we will generally call 'spirits'.

Spirits of the Spiritual Ecosphere

There are innumerable spirits. We shall classify them in two categories according to their positive or negative effect on the spiritual life of human beings.

Positive Spirits

Among the positive spirits, the most important one is the 'Face of God' or the absolute vali (Fig. 14).[1] The absolute vali is the absolute theophan, meaning that he reflects the totality of the Divine Essence. According to Ostad Elahi, there are different levels of theophanies:[2] 'An absolute theophany (a total manifestation of the Divine Essence) is different from a partial theophany (a partial manifestation of the Divine Essence).'[3] When the Face of God is present on earth in the form of the absolute vali, the latter is only known by a few people (his companions). The revolution of the Faces of God determines the revolutions of all the creatures, and each time the Divine Essence manifests itself in its totality in the terrestrial world, a new era begins. This change of era affects the entire Earth, and it is accompanied by a change in mentalities, cultures, knowledge, etc. The transition between two eras can last a century or more after the Face of God has departed from the Earth, but it is inescapable. In each era, the Face of God is unique and it differs from the others by the attributes it favours and the degree of those attributes.

After the Face of God come the 'facets', or valis,[4] who reflect the Face of God when it is not directly present in this world. The vali is a partial theophan; he is the representative of God on Earth, and the Earth is never devoid of one. The valis are among those who are called divine persons, all of whom are positive spirits. Among the divine persons are also the prophets, the great saints, etc, who may be partial theophans or not. Most of the divine persons are spiritual lords or companions of the Quiddity;[5] the prophets and valis necessarily have a mission. Finally, the souls of sincere believers are also included in this hierarchy of positive spirits, as are the souls of all those who are located at intermediate levels between sincere believers and divine persons.

It should be noted that when we talk about spirits, we

Figure 14　The Face of God

are referring to beings who are pure spirits and cannot be perceived by our ordinary senses. However, the Face of God and divine persons of high rank are powerful enough to have an influence on the spirits of human beings even when they are present on Earth.

Negative Spirits

Although negative spirits are quite numerous, in this study we shall examine only the two which human beings are most concerned with: saprophyte spirits and tempter spirits.

Saprophyte[6] spirits are spirits who live in our surroundings and who can see us and read our thoughts. They are harmless in and of themselves, but as soon as our spiritual immune system weakens, they are transformed into pathogenic spirits and attack us. Some of the factors which can disturb and weaken our spiritual immune system are real atheism, belief in a fictitious God, erroneous practice of a true belief, and the search for pseudo-spiritual pleasures and wonders. Saprophyte spirits become pathogenic when they express or actualize their inveterate hostility towards us and bring our thoughts under their influence. They can even go as far as entirely possessing our thoughts and making us think what they want us to think, meaning that, in spiritual matters, we take what is false to be true and what is true to be false.

Once they become pathogenic, the saprophyte spirits penetrate our thoughts through the channel of the imperious self. They strengthen pride, which results among other things in megalomania and greed for power; they also strengthen concupiscence, cupidity, aggressiveness, cunning, etc. By strengthening the negative traits of a human being, they tarnish his angelic soul, making it ill, lowering its vigilance and weakening or even totally annihilating its capacity to receive divine energy. In short, they turn the angelic soul into a wreck.

In general, people who are under the influence of these spirits are unaware of it, and they truly think that they are on the right path. As we have already said, saprophyte spirits attack human beings only if their spiritual immune system is already disrupted. The primordial substance of the angelic soul's spiritual immune system is pure faith in the true God.

Let us now move on to tempter spirits, who were created to test human beings. They are neither friends nor enemies, but they test us to see if we really deserve to advance and to rise higher or not. They stage extremely tempting situations for the imperious self, but in the guise of a pseudo-spiritual form and language. They are free to appear to human beings under any form they wish. Sometimes they appear to us through visions or in dreams, or through voices that we hear. They can also exert themselves directly upon our thoughts, without us even being aware of it, or indirectly, through the intermediary of another person.

It is through their words that one can recognize them as tempter spirits. Indeed, there is always a pathognomonic sign in their proposals which flatters the basharic side of human beings and reveals their trickery. For example, they can make someone believe that he is endowed with the mission of seizing power in order to save humanity, or that he is the Messiah and must free people from all prohibitions, etc. But in the tempting proposals of these spirits there is always a logical flaw that contradicts the principles of ethics and religion. Tempter spirits cross the path of all viators, as well as the path of anyone who prematurely ventures into the spiritual worlds without having prepared for it; to progress in the spiritual worlds, we must necessarily cross the zone of the tempter spirits.[7]

The Spiritual Environment

In an ecosystem, the environment is defined as 'the *ensemble* of factors which surround an organism and submit it to influences that have a bearing on its development, its physiology, its behaviour, etc, considering that these factors themselves are influenced by this organism in a necessary, specific and continuous exchange of actions and reactions'. One can distinguish between the macro-environment, which is the general environment, and the micro-environment. There are two kinds of factors which determine the environment: abiotic factors and biotic factors.[8] Similarly, the spiritual environment is formed of two kinds of factors: abiotic spiritual factors and biotic spiritual factors.

Abiotic Spiritual Factors

Radiations
Let us return for a moment to the biological cell. We know that in order to achieve its metabolism (consumption of energy, exchanges, nutrition), the cell needs energy. Some cells draw their energy from the decomposition of molecules, while other cells draw their energy from sunlight. The spiritual cell uses two kinds of energy: luminous radiation and spiritual molecules. The spiritual molecules are made up of several things, including our good intentions and actions – that is, actions we have performed in the direction of the Divine. As for luminous radiation, because nothing exists in creation without its opposite, there are two opposite sources of radiation in the spiritual ecosphere: divine light and negative radiation.

Negative radiation, which is absolutely to be avoided, comes from the 'fire' which emanates from the negative spirits; instead of supporting the cell's normal metabolism, this kind of radiation disrupts its proper functioning. As for the Divine Light, the self can receive it indirectly or directly through the intermediary of the vali, or a guide who was assigned a mission by the vali. The vali or the guide receives and regulates the Divine Energy and then transmits it to his students, as well as to all those who believe in his words. The Divine Energy is like a high-voltage line, and the vali – or the guide commissioned by the vali – is like a transformer: he allows us to receive the Divine Energy in a voltage that is appropriate for us.

When the guide does not have a mission from God, or when we do not have a guide, the self is unable to receive the Divine Energy properly. It is then forced to decompose its stored molecules and is consequently exposed to various hazards (fragility). There are other ways of receiving the Divine Energy, although they are less effective. These include prayers, and in general, anything that increases sincere faith.

Gravity (or The Forces of Attraction)
There are two forces of attraction which influence the environment of the spiritual ecosphere: the attraction of the metacausal world (divine entity) and the attraction of the causal world. For example, the presence of a divine person in a micro-environment increases the power of divine attraction and decreases the causal attraction in that environment.

The Spiritual Atmosphere
To understand the role that the atmosphere plays in the development of the spiritual cell, let us examine some concepts concerning cellular respiration. The cell needs oxygen, which it draws from its environment, to decompose the molecules that will provide it with energy. By means of that oxygen, the molecules[9] decompose into water and carbon dioxide, thereby liberating their energy; the carbon dioxide is then discarded. Similarly, for the self to achieve its metabolism, it too must draw its spiritual oxygen from the spiritual atmosphere. As in nature, spiritual oxygen is found everywhere, but this atmosphere can contain a great deal of pollution which is likely to disrupt the metabolism of the self – sometimes quite gravely.

In fact, every human being emits a gas into the atmosphere as a result of his or her spiritual respiration. This gas is different according to each individual. In the case of a divine person, this gas is oxygen; the more powerful the divine person's radiance, the greater the extent of the atmosphere that will be purified around him. In the case of a mere believer, the gas that is produced can be compared to a mixture of oxygen and carbon dioxide, whereas for a non-believer it is simply carbon dioxide. In the case of a venomous person,[10] it is pure carbon monoxide, a colourless and odourless gas that is highly toxic; hence, the danger of venomous persons, who can poison us without our even being aware of it. In addition to the gases that are emitted by human beings, the spiritual atmosphere can also be polluted by the negative actions, and more importantly, by the negative thoughts of human beings, which, like black smoke, hang heavy and thick on the atmosphere.

The spiritual atmosphere, then, may be quite polluted when the density of non-believers and negative individuals increases. This pollution weakens the angelic soul and can sometimes make it seriously ill. It is impossible for a human being to be in a neutral spiritual state. Indeed, according to the principle that everything is in motion, the human spirit is also in motion, in one direction or the other. If he does not do something to direct his movement towards a positive direction, a human being is bound to be subjected to the influence of his environment, which can pull him in a positive or negative direction – more likely in a negative direction considering today's world. Therefore, we must be vigilant and try to live in an unpolluted micro-environment, paying attention, for instance, to the kind of company we keep.

Temperature
The warmth of the spiritual environment comes from God.

However, as in the case of light, there is also a negative warmth which comes from the negative fire that is produced by people who are under the control of their imperious self; this fire is strengthened by the negative spirits. When the spiritual atmosphere is polluted, it acts as a screen between the Divine Source and human beings and prevents divine warmth from reaching them. The atmosphere freezes, and people who are deprived of Divine Warmth and Love turn towards the negative fire – excessive pleasures, carnal desires or pseudo-spiritual pleasures – which then assumes a disproportionate importance.

Water
Water is the divine teachings. When the teachings come from an authentic source, they are like pure water; when they come from an authentic source that has run dry, they are like stagnant water which, although still drinkable, provides very few benefits. Divine teachings that have degenerated and become permeated with human fantasies are comparable to polluted water. The absence of divine teachings is equivalent to a shortage of water. And spiritual teachings that emanate from a non-authentic source are like poisonous water.

Biotic Spiritual Factors

Biotic factors concern all of the relations which emerge between living beings in a given environment. Spiritual biotic factors are complex and numerous; here, we shall only examine the most significant.

Relations with Saprophyte and Tempter Spirits
Human beings who are confronted with saprophyte and tempter spirits can be classified into four main groups:

- The first group are those who seek pseudo-spiritual pleasures (visions, ecstasy . . .) while thinking that they are actually seeking Divine Love. When they enter the zone of tempter spirits, they are like inexperienced and gullible adolescents without any knowledge or protection who have ventured into a neighbourhood of streetwise delinquents. The tempter spirits will provide them with what they are looking for, but these pseudo-spiritual pleasures are comparable to the pleasures associated with drugs: they are fleeting, they give rise to dependency and a feeling of emptiness and ultimately they destroy the person.

- The second group are those who seek various kinds of inner peace or serenity, with or without the assistance of a master. It is not peace that they obtain, but rather a temporary inner anaesthesia, because they are looking for peace in the wrong place. As long as we are in the causal world, real peace is just a delusion, and the various techniques that are supposed to bring about serenity are in fact like tranquillizers; they artificially erase existential anguish or psychological problems of all kinds, but they simultaneously cause addiction. As soon as we stop using that particular technique, the problems and the anguish come back in an even more painful way.

- The third group are those who seek material-spiritual powers such as levitation, telekinesis, telepathy, instantaneous teleportation, etc. With or without the help of a guru and under the pretext of seeking spirituality, such people try to obtain powers which in fact come from nature itself or from pathogenic and tempter spirits. Although they obtain these powers for a more or less limited period of time, it only results in increasing their pride and ostentation and does not bring them anything spiritual.

- The fourth group are the genuine spiritual students. They are not after pleasure, anaesthesia, power or temporary serenity, but instead seek to know their rights and the duties they must carry out. They allow themselves to be guided by a divine laser ray, without stopping at useless amusements or paying attention to what might divert them from their goal. Following that ray, they safely cross the zone of the tempter spirits under the direct or indirect supervision of the God of the time.

Relations with Venomous Persons

Venomous human beings are people who are outwardly like you and me, but who are in fact quite toxic for those who, spiritually speaking, are still at the kindergarten or pre-school level. This matter deserves to have an entire study devoted to it, for among all the dangers that await people, this is the most pernicious. The venomous individual is a person who can divert you from authentic spirituality through his acts or words.

There are different kinds of venomous people. Suppose someone believes in God and one of his friends comes along and derides his faith, saying: 'How could you? In this day and age, is it still possible to believe in God? What is this really all about?' etc, and he succeeds in washing away all faith from the believer's heart and mind. Playing the role of a venomous person, that individual has poisoned the believer, without the latter even noticing it. The most venomous human beings are those who have committed so many vile and anti-divine actions that their soul has become black and has turned into a wreck; nothing spiritual remains in them, and they bear in their hearts, whether consciously or not, a genuine hatred for the Truth, destroying faith, morals, religions and true spirituality. Such venomous people generally appear very likeable, are pleasant and attractive and often hold a prominent status in society, so that their words carry a certain weight and do not raise any suspicions.

Relations with Divine Persons

Whether divine persons are present on the Earth or in the other world, it is always possible to establish relations with them. 'Each time we turn our attention towards spiritual persons, they are aware of it. And each time we implore them with faith, they come to our aid.'[11] If they are in the other world, it is enough to desire such a relation and to fulfil certain conditions, for example through pilgrimage or prayer, in order to establish communication. However, the grace that is enjoyed by having relations with a divine person on Earth is incomparable. A guide who has a mission from God is generally counted among the divine persons. As long as we live in the causal world, it is impossible to progress in any domain without committing errors and facing dangers unless we are helped by an authentic guide.

The authentic spiritual guide is a divine person of high rank who necessarily has a mission of guidance and helps those who trust him and sincerely believe in the true God. We have already seen the role that such a person plays in the transmission of Divine Light. To have such a guide has many advantages, but we will only mention a few. The guide has the right to favour his pupils. Those who believe in a revealed religion stand under a universal emblem; they stand in relation to their prophet as the inhabitants of a country would stand in relation to their king or president, meaning they are subject to the same general regulations as everyone else. The guide, on the other hand, acts like a father towards his children and has the right to take the particular situation of his pupil into account. Moreover, he protects his pupils against the various dangers and harmful energies. In fact, he creates a specific spiritual eco-system for his students which is extremely favourable to the development of their selves.

Relations with the Face of God
Beyond biotic and abiotic factors, the most determining factor in the spiritual environment is the Face of God. Why do we speak of the 'Face of God'? In fact, God is unique and He is multiple. He is unique in His essence and multiple in His manifestations, meaning His Faces or facets. The Faces of God are the direct manifestations of the Divine Essence under various forms and degrees, and it is only through the Face or the facets that creatures – namely, human beings – can accept and come to know the Creator.

Conclusion

It is extremely important to be conscious of the spiritual ecosphere's influence on our being, especially since the present ecosphere is unfavourable to spirituality, to say the least. We live in an ecosystem whose equilibrium has vanished, and signs of this are: the reversal of all values, the rise of indifference and selfishness, the loss of abundance, the increase of criminality and superficiality, the desertion of authentic religious sites, the spreading of cults etc. The spiritual atmosphere of our time is polluted indeed, and this pollution makes the soul feel apathetic, lazy and even depressed, to the point that it resents hearing about true spirituality.

Along with this weakening of the soul, the imperious self is automatically strengthened, which allows for negative spirits to reign. To resist the considerable influence of this environment, it is necessary to spend a considerable amount of energy, so it becomes imperative to receive the appropriate energy in the best way possible and to store up large reserves of molecules by acting in the direction of Divine Satisfaction. One should also remember that any factor, whether biotic or abiotic, has no influence upon us unless we are ready to receive its effect. So, if our receptor is defective, we might be among the people surrounding a divine person without ever benefiting from it. On the other hand, a spiritually advanced person may have shut down all of the receptors which could have exposed him to harmful influences; in other words, he has spiritually immunized himself.

Questions

Why does the absolute vali reveal himself to only a few people during his lifetime?

Because very few people can endure his light. If you plug a 1.5 volts, or even a 200 volts device into a high-voltage line of 300,000 volts, it will burn.

How many valis are there on Earth?

The general law is that they come one at a time.

Isn't this unjust for those who do not come to know him?

Every human being who sincerely seeks the vali will make contact with him, either directly or through the intermediary of his teachings.

According to you, who is the vali of our time?

That is like asking me where the sun is.

You have said that one cannot accept and then come to know God if not through the Face or the facets. Yet, many people believe in God without even being aware of their existence.

What I have been saying concerns the higher levels of

spirituality, the stages dealing with the 'knowledge of God'. At the elementary stages, things are different, and it is possible to have faith and to make progress without necessarily knowing the Face or a facet.

You say 'directly capture the divine light through the intermediary of the vali'. This somehow sounds contradictory to me . . .

The light that the vali reflects is the light of God; he is like a perfect mirror.

What place does Christ hold among your classification of positive spirits?

Christ was, among other things, the vali of his time. Today, whoever believes in him is considered a good citizen of the kingdom of Christ, and if that person's faith is sincere, Jesus Christ himself will guide that person and make him know what he needs to know.

What is the use of negative spirits in the order of creation?

If we manage to control them, negative spirits become rungs which enable us to climb part of the ladder leading to the metacausal world, but if they control us, they turn into a slippery slope which causes us to fall to the bottom of the ravine.

Why do you think venomous persons are dangerous? Isn't it easy to recognize them since they are destroying morals and religion?

Yes, but sometimes they can destroy them from the inside. Let us take an example: suppose one of them pretends to be a moralist and, under the cover of his authority, abrogates some moral rules and replaces them with others which are in fact against true morals. Because that person is an authority in the field, people take his pseudo-morals for real morals, and yet because they clearly see some inconsistencies in them, they end up rejecting morals altogether. Another example is that of religious hypocrites or fanatics who give a bitter image of what religion is. Venomous persons are all the more dangerous in that they are not conscious of their own state and think they are right.

You have not talked about angels. Don't they exist?

Angels are counted among the positive spirits.

Much is said nowadays about guardian angels . . .

Guardian angels exist, and for every family whose members are believers and united, God specially assigns a protecting angel. What we understand by 'angel' is a special kind of creature. There is a hierarchy among them. At the top are the archangels whom we call the 'spiritual lords'; they are the creatures closest to the Face of God, and they have, among other tasks, the mission of guiding people. Then there are other categories of angels . . .

How do you know all this?

As I have already said, everything that is spoken in these lectures is derived from the teachings of Ostad Elahi, teachings whose truth I have experienced after assimilating them and putting them into practice, at least sufficiently to understand their coherence and rationality. Ostad Elahi had gone, one by one, through all the stages that lead human beings to their goal, and every human being who reaches his goal knows himself, knows God and consequently knows all of creation.

Did Ostad Elahi himself have masters who educated him?

During his youth he had a master, but after that he was his own master.

Can you describe the process of spiritual respiration?

The soul breathes in the spiritual atmosphere just as a fish breathes in water.

You said that believers partially emit oxygen and that non-believers emit carbon dioxide. This is surprising, because you see many believers who do harm and many non-believers who are quite humane and honest. How do you explain that?

By 'believer', I mean someone who sincerely believes in the true original principles of divine religion, even without acknowledging their divine origin, and who practises the morals which derive from it. In any case, God's judgment is different from ours, for He has a complete view of things.

Why does God allow the atmosphere of the earth to become so frozen?

Like nature, the spiritual ecosphere has its seasons. Presently, it is winter; it is an exceptionally harsh winter, proportionate to the power of the Face of God of our era. But we will also have an exceptional spring.

---

[1] For a more detailed discussion on the subject of the vali, see PP, p. 216.

[2] Theophany: a divine manifestation. The theophan is a person in whom this manifestation takes place.

[3] AH 2, p. 110.

[4] The word 'vali' refers to the facets; the 'absolute vali' is the Face.

[5] See Study 3.

[6] Saprophyte: a medical term referring to something that lives in an

organism which is not pathogenic (causing disease), but which can become pathogenic under the influence of certain factors.

[7] This is not a zone in the physical sense, but a 'spiritual zone'.

[8] Abiotic factors are factors such as light, temperature, the chemical composition of water, etc. Biotic factors are determined by the presence of various organisms.

[9] Glucose molecules.

[10] Cf. infra.

[11] AH 2, p. 289.

Study 8

The Spiritual Immune System

Introduction. Exchanges between the Basharic Soul and the Angelic Soul. Biological Immunity. Definition; Distinguishing between the Self and the Non-Self; Antigens; Agents of the Immune Response; An example: Viral Infection. Malfunctionings: Deficiencies, Autoimmunity, Allergy, Vaccination and Serotherapy. **Spiritual Immunity.** Spiritual Antigens; the Spiritual Immune Response; Spiritual Allergies; Spiritual Autoimmunity; Spiritual Vaccination and Serotherapy. **Conclusion.**

Introduction

In the course of the preceding studies, we have made several references to these fundamental questions: 'Where do we come from? Why are we here? What must we do, and where are we going to?' (Fig. 15). I would like to return briefly to these questions in order to make it clear, at the end of this series of studies, what our essential duty as human beings is.

• First, where do we come from? We come from a spiritual realm or, if you prefer, from an immaterial one, and, within us, we carry the breath of the Divine Soul.

- Second, why are we here? To unite with our counterpart in order to acquire the potential to perfect ourselves. As we climb the ladder of causality, the intensity of causal determinism decreases, the more freedom we have and the more we are at peace.

- Third, what must we do? Being granted transcendent reason, willpower and the faculty of choice, we have a duty to climb, step by step, the ladder that crosses the causal worlds and allows us to reach the top, where we are eventually 'pulled up' by God Almighty, leaving the causal world for the metacausal world, the world of those who are perfect. We say 'pulled up by God Almighty' because before entering the world of the perfect beings, one has to cross a realm which is impossible to cross on one's own.

- Fourth, where are we going? When we have fulfilled ourselves, we return to our origin, having obtained total freedom and the capacity of absorbing with full consciousness the immeasurable graces that await us. As Ostad Elahi says: 'Whoever makes the required effort will reach his own perfection. At its lowest level, perfection consists in receiving from God all the sensations of joy and delight that exist in the whole of creation. It is indescribable; all we can say is that the sensations are continuously renewed and never repeat themselves, each new sensation being ever more delightful than the preceding one.'

Exchanges between the Basharic Soul and the Angelic Soul

As a follow-up to the analogy we have been sketching over the past three studies between the development of the soul and that of the cell, let me again say that as far as the

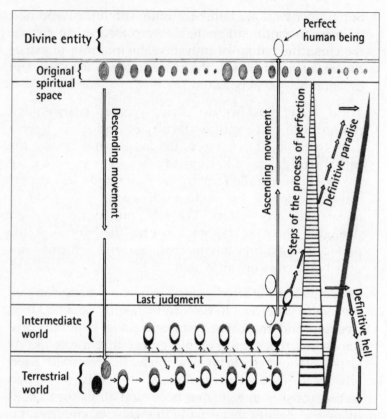

Figure 15   'Where do we come from? Why are we here? What must
we do? Where are we going?'

human being is concerned, the angelic soul (or celestial gamete) must combine with the basharic soul (or terrestrial gamete) to fulfil itself and to give birth to the spiritual zygote. We have also said that this was the indispensable condition for its perfection.

As for the biological cell, we have seen that two kinds of exchanges occur through the cellular membrane: passive exchanges and active exchanges. Passive exchanges follow simple physico-chemical laws; in a mechanical way, they automatically tend to establish an equilibrium between the solutions on both sides of the membrane. In active exchanges, the cell constantly challenges these physico-chemical laws as it actively interferes in the exchanges.

In the same way, one could say that exchanges between the two gametes, terrestrial and celestial, are at once both passive and active. Since there is a higher concentration of molecules (characteristics) from the terrestrial gamete, if the celestial gamete remains passive, the excess molecules present in the basharic soul invade the angelic soul. These characteristics of the terrestrial gamete are strengthened, as we have said, by external forces. When the characteristics of the basharic soul are present in excess in the angelic soul, the latter becomes insensitive to anything related to authentic spirituality; it becomes weaker and progressively suffocates because it cannot receive the Divine (Divine Light and Warmth). This is the reason why the angelic soul must play a very active role in the regulation of these exchanges. It must act by itself and regulate the permeability of its membrane to prevent the invasion of excess basharic characteristics; it must also immunize itself against the invading characteristics, allowing each characteristic to enter only in necessary doses. In fact, to regulate the exchanges properly, the angelic soul must be healthy, and to remain healthy, it must immunize itself. If we want to understand this process of immunization, it is necessary to review briefly some points about the immunity of the human body.

Biological Immunity

Definition

In biology, immunity refers to all the mechanisms which help to maintain the integrity of the individual in his environment. It is the aptitude, then, to recognize and control a prodigious number of aggressors called antigens.

Distinguishing between the Self and the Non-Self

Normally, if it wants to fulfil its function, the immune system must first distinguish between the self and the non-self. Generally speaking, the immune system considers all molecules that do not belong to the individual as foreign (non-self) and reacts against them; on the other hand, it recognizes the molecules belonging to the individual (self) and does not react against them.

Antigens

Anything that is recognized as non-self by the organism and that is capable of generating a response by the immune system is an antigen. An antigen is an organic substance that can come from outside the organism, or it can be a molecule from the organism itself that has become foreign, meaning that it has taken on the characteristics of the non-self. Antigens can thus have an external origin (bacteria, viruses, etc) or an internal origin (a modified molecule from the organism).

Agents of the Immune Response

The body's immune system has many defenders at its disposal to face antigens. These defenders are the immune cells (lymphocytes, macrophage tissue cells, etc). The immune cells fulfil several functions:

• they recognize potentially pathogenic agents (antigens);
• they neutralize these agents;

- they eliminate such agents (kill and phagocytize); and
- they memorize the characteristics of an agent in order to react more rapidly if it reappears in the future.

In the course of the immune response, some immune cells (lymphocytes) produce molecules named antibodies; these antibodies have the property of specifically combining with the antigen that triggered their synthesis in order to neutralize that antigen, marking them so they can be phagocytized by macrophages. They also provide the memory which is necessary for defending the body against subsequent attacks of the same antigen.

An Example: Viral Infection

We have seen that viruses are antigens. Viruses are specific pathogenic agents that can only multiply in living cells which they infect. The virus penetrates the cell, merges with the cell's genetic material and consequently alters the cell's metabolism. The infected cell then begins to produce viral proteins that assemble into mini-viruses, which in turn invade the cell, destroy it and go on to another cell. This is called viral infection. Having identified the aggressors, the organism then synthesizes antibodies which ensure that the viral infection is neutralized and controlled.

Malfunctionings of the Immune System

Deficiencies

Many factors are likely to weaken the immune system. For example, since antibodies are protein molecules, a malnourished person does not have sufficient protein reserves to produce enough antibodies; consequently, such

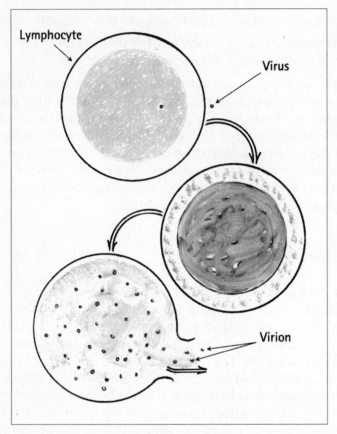

Figure 16   Viral infection

a person will be more frail when facing an attack. Other circumstances can also alter the efficiency of the immune system: pregnancy, growth, convalescence, precarious diet/hygienic conditions, depression, environment, age, etc.

Autoimmunity
The distinction between the self and the non-self is obvious

as long as it is a foreign agent that attacks the human organism. But in certain circumstances or under unfavourable conditions, the normally cognizant immune system may sometimes be disrupted and may turn against its own organism. This is called autoimmunity – the production of antibodies which react against one or several components of the organism itself, mistaking them for foreign agents. Autoimmunity is thus at the origin of a number of 'autoimmune diseases', such as insulin-dependent diabetes, in which antibodies destroy the pancreatic cells that normally produce insulin, a hormone essential to the metabolism of sugars.

Allergy
It sometimes happens that the immune system overreacts when it encounters an antigen it has previously been sensitized to; it is a type of hypersensitivity. An allergy is therefore an excessive response to an otherwise typical exposure to a given antigen.

Vaccination and Serotherapy
It is possible to strengthen the immune system, particularly through vaccination and serotherapy. Vaccination involves introducing into the body antigens that have been rendered harmless, triggering a synthesis of neutralizing antibodies; in other words, generating the development of functional antibodies able to prevent aggression. Serotherapy involves injecting a serum that already contains antibodies specific to one or several antigens, directly providing efficient protection against aggression.

Spiritual Immunity

Having defined these biological concepts, let us return to our analogy between the spiritual dimension and the physical dimension of human beings. Parallel to the body, the soul has its own spiritual immune system, whose aim is to maintain the soul's integrity against spiritual antigens which threaten to attack it, weaken it or make it ill and disrupt its growth.

Spiritual Antigens

Spiritual antigens originate from two sources: the primary source is intrinsic, the secondary source extrinsic. The intrinsic spiritual antigens come from the excesses of the worker self – ie, avid and apathetic drives. When the worker self is not controlled by our transcendent reason, it falls into disorder and disequilibrium – either excess or insufficiency – as it does not know its limits. It then manifests itself as the 'imperious self',[1] attacking and intoxicating the soul. Consider, for instance, the instinct of attracting benefit. When it becomes excessive, it engenders envy, greed etc, which are toxic for the soul. This disruption of the worker self is a result of a deficiency in the spiritual immune system.

To attack and invade the angelic soul, the imperious self is also strengthened by extrinsic negative energy.[2] The receivers of this negative energy are the avid and apathetic drives. An avid drive is an uncontrolled surge of the worker self's desires (excess). An apathetic drive, on the other hand, is one which is opposed to passions (insufficiency) and which manifests itself as a total or partial lack of motivation and desire (depression, suicide etc). In other words, as long as the worker self is under the control of our transcendent reason and does not go beyond its limits, extrinsic negative energy does not have any effect on us. Finally, the imperious self also needs catalysts. Biological catalysts are substances that favour and accelerate physico-chemical reactions. In the case of the self, different factors can play the role of spiritual catalysts, especially people and society. Once again, the role of extrinsic energy and catalysts demonstrates the importance of the environment and education in the process of the self's development.

Extrinsic spiritual antigens are the micro-organisms (viruses, bacteria etc) and toxins that are emitted from negative spirits, whether human or non-human. Among the most dangerous spiritual micro-organisms and poisons for the soul are human beings who have been spiritually contaminated. Indeed, they behave like pathogenic viruses. Their spirits penetrate the thoughts of human beings and alter the 'genetic code' of their transcendent reason, which consequently loses its faculty of distinguishing right from wrong; thus, it takes right for wrong and wrong for right. Those who are contaminated in this manner contaminate others in turn.

The Spiritual Immune Response

Like the body, the soul has a set of mechanisms that allow it to fight against aggression and to maintain its integrity. The main difference is that we ourselves must take care of our spiritual immune system, at least during the first stage, which we call the pre-automatic period. In the second stage, when our spiritual immune system has been properly tuned, it functions by itself in an automatic way: this is called the automatic period.

During the pre-automatic period, the soul must first educate itself in terms of how to distinguish self from non-self, so that it can recognize spiritual antigens. It will be able to make that distinction when it knows the authentic divine principles and precepts brought to it by the divine messengers who have been entrusted with a mission and who bear the divine seal. For example, divine messengers teach us that our true nature consists in respecting the rights of others. Thus, if we feel aggressive or greedy drives within us that lead us to infringe upon the rights of others, we must consider them as non-self.

The soul must then learn how to produce specific spiritual antibodies. To produce these antibodies, the soul must first gather the materials that will enable it to build and operate the cells which specialize in the synthesis of these antibodies. To make the process of the functioning of the soul's immune cells more palpable, one may compare it with micro-factories. The materials for the construction of these micro-factories are the intentions and actions that we carry through as duties, aiming for Divine satisfaction. For every antigen, there is a micro-factory that specializes in the production of the specific corresponding antibodies, because *'Just as the remedy for each illness of the body is in the body itself, the remedy for each illness of the soul is also found in the soul itself.'*[3]

Each time the soul has finished building a micro-factory (cell), it must receive the divine seal in order for this micro-factory to work in an automatic way and on a permanent basis. For as soon as the factory has been built and is in working order – thanks to the divine seal – it is endowed with a faculty that automatically produces the specific antibodies. So, not only is there a pre-automatic and an automatic period for the spiritual immune system as a whole, but the same is also true for each of the micro-factories in this system.

It is not enough, however, to build the factory; it must also be provided with raw materials. The soul must draw the raw materials necessary for the production of spiritual antibodies from the worker self. It is clear, therefore, that the worker self is more than just the basis of the imperious self; it also plays an essential role in the immunization of the soul by providing the raw materials for the production of antibodies, and, in small doses, the antigenic substances necessary for the soul to vaccinate itself. This is one of the reasons why we should avoid everything that may harm the worker self, such as asceticism or addiction, and instead be concerned with maintaining our bodies in good health.

Both the imperious self and the angelic soul, therefore, draw their primary substances from the worker self. Out of these primary substances, the imperious self produces toxins which act against the soul, and the soul produces specific antibodies which protect it. However, whereas the imperious self produces its toxins automatically, in an instinctive and innate manner, the angelic soul must gain a certain knowledge to produce its antibodies, because it has to manage the development of its immune system *by itself* and by its own choice. This difference is naturally due to the faculty of the angelic soul that we call transcendent reason.

The process of the soul's immune response must be coordinated by transcendent reason and closely supervised by the God of the time Himself, either directly or indirectly. The assistants of transcendent reason are the consciences (blaming, inspiring and certifying) and the executive reason. To support and accelerate the process of immunization, the angelic soul needs two other elements: positive energy and catalysts.

The source of positive energy is God. As for the catalysts, different factors can play this role, especially positive people and a favourable environment. However, the substrate of the soul's immunization is a pure and sincere faith in the true God (the God of the time). Faith comes into play at all levels: through faith, the transcendent reason can fulfil its function as coordinator; faith acts as a barrier against intrinsic and extrinsic aggressors, programming the genetic code of spiritual molecules formed by our intentions and positive actions (this code allows for the production of spiritual antibodies); faith is the receiver that enables the soul to pick up the positive energy that it needs, etc.

To illustrate the importance of a sincere faith in the true God, we can take the example of diamonds and graphite (used for pencil leads). Diamonds and graphite are both made up of identical carbon atoms, the only difference being the arrangement of their atoms: a diamond is a structure that holds through four perfect covalent bonds, whereas only three of the four bonds are covalent in graphite (Fig. 17).

Going back to the soul, we could say that sincere faith in the true God attracts divine help. It is His help that enables us to produce spiritual diamonds from the raw material of carbon atoms, so that little by little we can transform ourselves into living diamonds. But if we do not have faith, or if our faith is insincere, or if our God is not true, then there is no Divine help; we are left alone to arrange our carbon atoms and, instead of producing diamonds, we produce graphite, which blackens our self and then goes on to contaminate and blacken the souls of others.

Let us now illustrate the process of spiritual immunization using the example of jealousy. Jealousy is a toxin which first attacks our own soul. According to Ostad Elahi, 'Jealousy is like an acid that first attacks the heart of the jealous person himself before reaching the person who is the object of jealousy.'

Using the same method of analogy, let us consider a simple chemical formula:

$$HCl + NaOH \rightarrow NaCl + H_2O$$

In other words, the association of hydrochloric acid (HCl) and caustic soda (NaOH), which consists of sodium and water, produces common table salt (NaCl) and water (H_2O)). One could compare jealousy to hydrochloric acid. To fight against that acid (antigen) which tends to take over, the soul must draw sodium and water from the

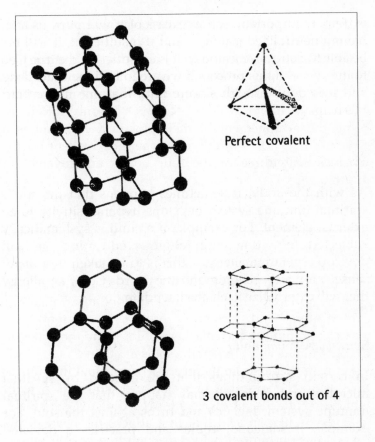

Perfect covalent

3 covalent bonds out of 4

Figure 17   Diamond and graphite

worker self, combine them in one of its micro-factories and produce caustic soda. This caustic soda (antibody) will enable the soul to neutralize the hydrochloric acid, which represents jealousy in this analogy. Moreover, this chemical reaction will produce elements that are beneficial to life, such as table salt and water, which in the case of jealousy translates into emulation and clemency.

The dose of caustic soda that the soul produces is

extremely important, for an excess of it will burn us after having neutralized jealousy, and if insufficient, it will not be able to neutralize jealousy. It is essential for the true God to intervene in this process if we are to find the exact dose, and it is only through sincere faith that one may attract His help.

Spiritual Allergy

As with the body, it sometimes happens that the soul's spiritual immune system develops hypersensitivity to an external element. For example, if a child is systematically subjected to a dogmatic religious education, he will develop a genuine allergy – this is to be taken in a literal sense – towards religion and the word 'God', an allergy that will externalize itself at a later date.

Spiritual Autoimmunity

In certain surroundings that are affected by spiritual microbes and toxins, it may happen that the spiritual immune system deviates and turns against the soul. For example, if someone studies and practises a deviated spirituality, his spiritual immune system takes the self to be the non-self and subsequently produces auto-antibodies which directly attack the soul.

Spiritual Vaccination and Serotherapy

Every guide who is a true spiritual physician has the power of spiritually vaccinating his students when he deems it necessary. If they can, students also have a duty to vaccinate themselves against temptations. Pathological anger, for instance, is a genuine poison (toxin) for the soul and the body. Ostad Elahi says: 'If someone who is under the influence of pathological anger controls himself with the help of God and succeeds in concealing it, he will gradually vaccinate himself and end up mastering his anger.' For that vaccination to be successful, several elements are needed: the support of the God of the time and sincerity towards Him, on the one hand, and will-power and faith, on the other.

Let us consider another very simple example, that of someone who has a weakness for television and cannot stop watching it even when he has something important to do. Such a person must gradually vaccinate himself against this weak point. To do so, he can designate a certain amount of time daily to watch television and resolve to adhere to that time. Whenever he fails to do this, he may deprive himself of watching television for one day.

There is also spiritual serotherapy. The God of the time, as well as a guide who has been entrusted with a mission by Him, can inject a serum containing antitoxins into a student who needs it. Many elements can also play the role of a serum, such as prayers, pilgrimages, a favourable environment etc.

Conclusion

Before ending this lecture, I would like to draw your attention to this essential point. We human beings necessarily play a voluntary role in the coordination of our spiritual immune system's various mechanisms during the pre-automatic period. Even if we want to, it is impossible for us to remain static, because we are constantly being attacked by internal and external aggressors. Remaining static is impossible anyway: if we are not progressing, then we are regressing.

We are all either consciously or unconsciously swept away by the currents of causality and by the passive exchanges between the soul and the body, so if the angelic soul remains passive, it is heading for disaster. Conversely, if it makes progress, the body gradually assumes the soul's colour: the divine particle pervades the whole person and the whole body (Fig. 18). It is at that moment that we see and know God, because we see God in ourselves. Being endowed with reason and free will, we have the duty to inform ourselves at the right source and receive the instructions that will enable us to coordinate all the means at our disposal for the preservation of our spiritual health, and thus to progress in the right direction. Now, to advance in the right direction, we must bear in mind a few fundamental concepts:

- First, the essential task of the soul on earth is to struggle constantly against the antigens (toxins) of the imperious self in order to synthesize the antibodies necessary for acquiring total and eternal spiritual immunity.

- Second, we must remember that the realm of the body is a gift from the Creator to the soul, so that the soul may use it as a counterpart and fulfil itself.

- Third, what remains of us and lives eternally is our angelic soul. It is therefore the angelic soul and not the imperious self which will have to answer for our actions on the Day of Judgment. If, after all its struggles, the soul succeeds in mastering the imperious self, glory and joy await it; if it lets the imperious self defeat it, however, its lot will be nothing but remorse and shame.

Our spiritual goal is to produce antibodies or antitoxins that will fight against all conceivable spiritual antigens. But what we must achieve through our free will is only a small part of our work towards perfection, a small part which is in fact proportionate to our freedom. If we manage to

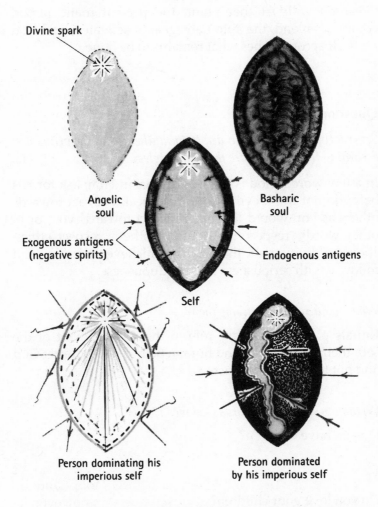

Divine spark

Angelic soul

Basharic soul

Exogenous antigens
(negative spirits)

Endogenous antigens

Self

Person dominating his
imperious self

Person dominated
by his imperious self

Figure 18   Sketch of the soul's process of immunization

perform our task, we will become totally conscious of our 'nothingness'. And as soon as we reach that state of 'nothingness', we enter the stage of submission to the

Creator's will. At that point, the pre-automatic period comes to an end, the automatic gear is activated, and God Himself accomplishes what remains to be done.

Questions

Several times you have alluded to the authentic divine principles; according to you, what are those principles?

In a few words: God is unique; believe in Him; ask for His help; do not think evil and do not speak evil; act towards others as you would like others to act towards you, or in other words, respect the rights of others; respect ethics; choose a divine path that is just, whichever you like, and follow it with seriousness and assiduousness.

What about religious rituals then?

Rituals play a secondary role in the development of the self; their aim is to remind human beings not to forget God and not to commit base acts.

What does sincerity towards God mean?

Do you have children?

Yes.

Do you love your children?

Yes.

You love them sincerely. Love God in exactly the same way. Everything that is good, you want for your children; you are ready to sacrifice everything for their sake. That is what is meant by sincerity.

You have talked about allergies and you have given the example of children who receive a dogmatic religious education. What do you mean by a dogmatic religious education?

In their own time, the prophets, whom I call spiritual scientists or spiritual physicians, had such an impact that their message seemed obvious, and those who listened to them did not feel the need for any explanations. After the prophets departed from this world, their disciples wished to carry on their teachings. People started to ask questions. Instead of admitting that they did not know the answers, their disciples tried to answer them and provided explanations that one might call 'intellectual' explanations. One who teaches spirituality, however, must not rely on his mind alone; he needs a certain spiritual insight as well. By relying exclusively on the mind, one necessarily wanders from the real truth. The framework of the principles remains true, but it has been obscured by intellectual interpretations that have turned these principles into dogmas.

What can we do to prevent a child from developing such an allergy towards religion?

We have to teach children a pure spirituality adapted to their own level. We have to encourage them without forcing them, and we ourselves have to practise the principles that are taught, so that gradually children may become familiar with the taste of spirituality.

Can you provide examples of diseases of the soul?

Real atheism, doubt, the drive towards immoral actions, spiritual asthenia etc. 'Among spiritual illnesses,' Ostad Elahi says, 'one of the most serious, painful and dangerous is doubt. Very few spiritual physicians can cure it. Pride and doubt are cancers of the soul.'[4]

But if one does not doubt, isn't there a risk of falling into the hands of simply anyone?

As long as one has not found a true divine teaching, doubt is a good thing because that kind of doubt is constructive. But as soon as one has found such a teaching, one must stop doubting, for doubt can become a serious disease if it still continues at that stage.

How does one fight against jealousy?

Fighting jealousy requires us, through auto-suggestion, to be kind, affectionate and nice towards the person we are jealous of. If you try it, you will realize that it is so difficult that it burns, like caustic soda. It is necessary for that process to take place under the direction of a guide, for if the dose of 'anti-jealousy' is too high, it may generate complexes and repressions.

You seem to be opposed to asceticism, but isn't it a necessary stage in the liberation of the soul, which, after all, is the goal of ascetic mysticism?

The ascetic weakens and mortifies his body in order to dry up the source of his imperious self's drives. He manages to free his soul from the grip of the body. But at what cost? First and foremost, he acts contrary to the divine principles. No authentic prophet has ever recommended mortification or asceticism as a technique for liberating the soul. In addition, he commits a grave error in that his body has been entrusted to him by God, and asceticism is a betrayal of that trust. He infringes upon the rights of his body, a wholly exceptional creature considering that it is the outcome of the perfection of matter, and which therefore has as many rights as the soul.

Moreover, by allowing his worker self to deteriorate, the

ascetic annihilates the aggressors and thus deprives his angelic soul of the possibility of immunizing itself against them. Furthermore, by suppressing the very source of the raw materials of the micro-factories that produce antibodies, he denies his angelic soul the possibility of immunizing itself against external aggressors as well. In short, he is totally disarmed. For example, if a watchdog barks too much, one could always let it starve so as to weaken it to the point of not barking any more, but at the same time, this would open the way for burglars and thieves. In other words, the ascetic impedes his own fulfilment. We are here on Earth to fulfil ourselves, and the body is the essential complement towards this end. The ascetic annihilates the effects of the body, and his soul returns to the state it was in before it entered the body. But if that was the goal, what would be the use of our coming to Earth in the first place? It would mean that God's ways are absurd.

Another reason for our coming to Earth is to establish a spiritual 'pension' for ourselves in anticipation of our eternal life. Now the ascetic who seeks visions, paranormal states, wonders etc, wastes his income to receive such things, and eventually all that remains is an addiction to these kinds of drugs or spiritual entertainment. Earth is the place where we should sow, not reap.

Naturally, some mystics have truly purified their selves through asceticism, but the aim of human beings is perfection. Although perfection implies purification, it mostly consists of maturing or perfecting our understanding. This maturation cannot be obtained by weakening the imperious self; on the contrary, it is by strengthening the imperious self along with the soul that the latter can master the former. A strong soul is a soul that dominates a strong imperious self, not a soul that has no imperious self against which to pit itself. Ostad Elahi says: 'This method of struggling against the imperious self is like a new medicine which required many years of ascetic practice, experimentation and research before I developed it and understood it.'[5]

Ostad Elahi practised asceticism during the first third of his life, and then experimented with a new kind of spirituality, natural spirituality, which respects the rights of every thing including the body. Because he had experimented with both methods, he understood the points that I have just explained and concluded that if asceticism may be a method for silencing the imperious self, it is by no means a method for achieving perfection.

When I perform an action, how can I judge my true intention?

If we really look within ourselves, we know whether our intention is good or bad. But it is still possible for us to make errors in our judgment. To avoid such errors, your judgments must have a sound basis, meaning that they must be founded upon authentic principles of divine origin.

How can the body assume the colour of the soul?

The colour of the soul is transparent. When the body assumes the soul's colour, it becomes qualitatively transparent, and what is true of the body is true of each particle of that body. The incorruptibility of some bodies can be explained by the same phenomenon.

Some people are immunized against certain temptations or bad types of behaviours, without having expended any effort. Is there something like innate immunity?

It is an immunity that was acquired during preceding lives, because we keep what we have acquired from one life to the next.

According to what you say, for absolutely everything that we set out to do in spirituality, we need a guide. But how can we reach maturity if we are constantly dependent?

As long as we are in this causal world, we are dependent upon causes; if we can go up one floor without using stairs, then we can say we are not dependent on stairs.

Another element that seems essential if we want to progress without danger is sincere faith in the true God. I personally do not have that sincere faith in the true God. Does this mean I cannot do anything without facing danger?

If you have faith, regardless of how weak it may be, and if you put it into practice according to the right principles, it will grow into a sincere faith, and it may even lead you to certitude – that is, you will know and even see the true God.

You have spoken of viruses which contaminate people. Are there epidemics of spiritual diseases?

Yes. But unfortunately, we are far beyond the stage of epidemics; we should talk about pandemics. People are so indoctrinated and so conditioned by false principles that they are completely lost, disoriented, and can no longer distinguish between true principles of divine origin and false principles.

Are you more pessimistic or optimistic about the future?

From a spiritual point of view, I am very optimistic about the future of humanity because humanity has God on its side, and because God is merciful and does not punish us if we do not understand; He prefers to make us understand things. I can only hope that He will make us understand those things in a gentle way . . . I think that for a few decades we will continue going towards ignorance, until our ignorance reaches a point of saturation. When our ignorance is saturated, God will gently take our hand, as if we were children, and He will show us the truth.

---

[1] Regarding the excesses and insufficiencies of the worker self, see the analysis of the terrestrial gamete in Study 6.

[2] Or by negative radiation. See 'The Spiritual Environment' in Study 7.

[3] AH 2, p. 36.

[4] AH 2, p. 30.

[5] AH 1, p. 267.

Bibliography

Ostad Elahi, *100 maximes de Guidance*, Paris, Robert Laffont, 1995, 158 pages; illustrations by André Marzuk
English edition: *100 Maxims of Guidance*, Paris, Robert Laffont, 1995
—*Confidences: Prières d'Ostad Elahi*, Paris, Robert Laffont, 1995, 48 pages; illustrations by Charles Hossein Zenderoudi
English edition: *Words of Faith: Prayers of Ostad Elahi*, Paris, Robert Laffont, 1995
Bahram Elahi, *La Voie de la Perfection*, Paris, Albin Michel, 4th ed., 1992, 234 pages
English edition: *The Path of Perfection*, Shaftesbury, Element Books, 3rd ed., 1996
—*Le chemin de la Lumière*, Paris, Albin Michel, 1985, 220 pages
English edition: *The Way of Light*, Shaftesbury, Element Books, 1993
—*Actes du symposium 'Le Spirituel: Pluralité et Unité'*, Paris, Presses Universitaires de Paris–Sorbonne, 1996, 196 pages
—*La Musique céleste d'Ostad Elahi*, Compact disc, Le Chant du Monde, 1996
—*Vie et oeuvre d'Ostad Elahi*, Video tape of the exhibition 'Vie et oeuvre d'Ostad Elahi', Paris, Chapelle de la Sorbonne, 1995 (English version: *Life and Work of Ostad Elahi*, Welcome Distribution, 1996)

Glossary

Abiotic spiritual factors: factors which form the spiritual environment: radiation (divine light and negative radiation), spiritual gravitation, spiritual atmosphere, spiritual temperature and spiritual water.

Absolute theophan (or absolute vali): a *positive spirit** who is a total manifestation of the divine essence.

Angelic soul (or celestial gamete): the soul coming directly from one of the three *spiritual spaces.** In human beings, it is formed of two essential components: the *divine spark** and *reason.** According to its capacity, it can be more or less lofty, brilliant and powerful, but before uniting with its complement, the *basharic soul,** it lacks any specific form or concrete consciousness and does not have the freedom to leave its original space.

Animal spirit or soul: the vital essence which bestows life upon and animates the process of perfection of an animal.

Apathetic drive: a drive of the *imperious self** opposite to that of the passions, manifesting itself through a lack of motivation and willpower.

Archangels: the highest creatures after God's *total essence.*

Ascending successive lives: a theory clearly set forth by Ostad Elahi, stating the existence of successive lives for each individual. Its characteristics are the following: a limited number of bodies, the obligation for the human soul to go to the *interworld** before receiving a new body, and above all, the fact that the soul's movement is in an ascending direction, meaning that, apart from certain exceptions, the soul cannot regress to an inferior stage in the course of its normal development.

Automatic period of the spiritual immune system: the period during which the *spiritual immune system** functions in an automatic way.

Avid drive: an uncontrolled surge of desires of the *imperious self.**

Basharic soul (or terrestrial gamete): the angelic soul's complement, it is the end point of the process of perfection of the mineral, vegetal and animal souls, and consequently bears within itself mineral, vegetal and animal properties. It has two components: the *worker self** and the *imperious self.**

Biotic spiritual factors: the relations between human beings and the different spirits of the *spiritual ecosphere.**

Blaming conscience: a faculty of *transcendent reason** that is the voice of conscience within us. It blames us when we have acted, or are about to act, contrary to *morality.**

Causal universe: all the cosmos (the physical world) together with the causal spiritual worlds.

Celestial gamete: see *angelic soul.*

Celestial reason: That which knows how to maintain an equilibrium between the requirements of material life and spiritual life, or in other words, between the four pillars of existence: this world, the other world, our soul and our body.

Certifying conscience: a faculty of the *transcendent reason** which produces in human beings the certitude of having acted in conformity with divine satisfaction, manifesting itself through a deep feeling of joy which is inexplicable in material terms and which is sometimes called 'a clear conscience'.

Characteristic ingredients of the soul: characteristics of the angelic soul dissolved in its constituent substance, such as rectitude, sincerity, love of honour and glory, as well as naiveté, excessiveness, ignorance, an attraction towards spiritual pleasures etc.

Concupiscent faculty: a faculty of appetance belonging to the *basharic soul** which in excess generates *stomachic love,** lust and other appetites such as greed, jealousy, the search for pleasure, etc. When it is insufficient, it generates lack of appetite, asthenia, depression etc; in equilibrium it generates decency and restraint.

Constituent substance of the soul: dignity.

Creational factors of the human being: the factors which determine the physical, psychological and spiritual aptitudes of the individual. There are seven factors: individual genetic effects, compositional genetic effects, the thoughts of the parents at the moment of conception, nutrition, time and place, education and socio-cultural environment, and the divine will.

Determined duties: an instinctive action accomplished by a creature in order to achieve its *potential rights.**

Divine entity: see *metacausal world*.

Divine person: a *positive spirit** who has a high spiritual rank (eg, prophets, great saints, etc).

Divine regard: exceptional attentiveness bestowed by the *Face of God** on something or someone; it is always beneficial.

Divine seal: a divine stamp which authenticates everything that God approves.

Divine spark (or divine breath): the effect of the breath of the Divine Soul.

Essential reality of a being: what a being really is, its *real truth.**

Eternal memory: memory belonging to the metaphysical dimension of human beings, which records absolutely everything and exists as long as the soul exists.

Ethics: the practice of *morality.**

Evil: complications brought about by responsible beings through ill use of their free will.

Executive reason: one of the aspects of *reason** (the other being *transcendent reason**). It is in charge of executing the commands of the transcendent reason and selects the means through which to do so.

Face of God: The total essence of God taking form. Each form varies according to the attributes that God allows to be manifested to the creatures during a given era. The Face of God manifests itself in the *absolute theophan.**

Facet of God: a *divine person** or *vali** who reflects the *Face of God** when the latter is not present on Earth.

Free duty: duty which requires training and willpower to be accomplished.

Genetics of the soul: a study of the characteristics that the soul inherits from its preceding lives, and from the *creational factors.**

God of the time: the *Face of God** of each era.

Gravitational force of the divine entity: the attraction exerted by the *metacausal world** on the *causal world.**

Imaginative faculty: a faculty of the *basharic soul** which enables us to envision the details and particulars of things; it naturally generates cunning, trickery, deception, fear etc, but, when under the control of the *executive reason,** it generates ingenuity and prudence.

Imperious self: one of the two components of the *basharic soul** (the other being the *worker self**). An internal hyperactive reasoning power which, when uncontrolled, leads us to do evil. The imperious self is the manifestation of destructive, ferocious and predatory animal characteristics in disequilibrium. It is rebellious, stubborn and intrusive.

Inspiring conscience: a faculty of the *transcendent reason** which inspires us as to what is good or right and what is bad or false, as long as it is not faulty or subjected to interference.

Interworld: the intermediate world between the cosmos and the spiritual worlds, located in the atmosphere of each planet. When they are not on their planet, it is the provisional residence for souls that have yet to reach the end of the time-limit set for their perfection.

Irascible faculty: a faculty of anger belonging to the *basharic soul** which in excess engenders predation, aggression, transgression, oppression etc. In equilibrium, it engenders firmness, courage and a sense of honour.

Material complements: material creatures which, through their necessary union, generate a new and complete material being apt for development (eg, the female gamete and the male gamete).

Mental self: the self in its ordinary material condition, made of the body, the intellect and the psyche.

Metacausal universe or world (or divine entity): the world that is not governed by the law of causality; it is the place of beings who have rejoined God.

Metacausal world: see *metacausal universe*.

Mineral spirit or soul: the vital essence which bestows life upon and animates the process of perfection of a mineral.

Morality: the science of good and evil derived from the divine source.

Natural spirituality: a spirituality based on the knowledge and application of the rights and duties assigned by the Creator. It is adapted to the nature of the soul and is capable of nourishing the spirit of human beings in a healthy manner, thus ensuring the progressive maturation and normal growth of the spirit until it reaches its fulfilment, or in other words, until it reaches *total concrete consciousness*.*

Necessary potential right: a *necessary right** which a creature must obtain on its own by carrying out its appropriate duties.

Necessary right: a means granted by the Creator to enable a creature to benefit from its *primordial right*.*

Necessary universal innate right: a *necessary right** granted from the outset to all creatures.

Negative spirit: a spirit which has a negative influence on the soul and the human psyche.

Ordinary clairvoyance: a faculty which is inherent in certain individuals, independent from their faith, spiritual level and will, which allows them to see and foretell some ordinary things in a more or less clear and exact manner.

Original contract: the contract that the representatives of human beings entered into with God in the world of particles at the time He created man; it refers to the rights and duties of human beings and is periodically renewed by the *Face of God** of the time.

Original space of the soul: an infinite space created prior to the planets; the source of souls and all creatures.

Partial theophan: a *positive spirit** who is a partial manifestation of the divine essence.

Positive spirit: a spirit who has a positive influence on the soul and the human psyche.

Pre-automatic period of the spiritual immune system: the period during which human beings must regulate their *spiritual immune system** by themselves.

Primordial matter: primary matter created by God simultaneously with the *Quiddity.**

Primordial right: the right of each creature that comes into existence to reach the goal for which it has been created, or in other words, the right to benefit fully from the divine grace, in proportion to its capacity.

Pure and sincere faith in God: pure faith is to see only God, to believe only in God and to rely only on Him. Sincere faith is to love God for God's sake, to love Him more than anyone else, even more than oneself.

Quiddity (Total Soul): the first creation and the manifestation of God.

Quintessence of all religions: all the pure, original principles derived from the divine source and revealed by the divine messengers, as elucidated by Ostad Elahi.

Real truth: a truth that corresponds to an objective truth which leads us to certitude – that is, to the verification of its reality.

Reason: one of the components of the *angelic soul** (the other being the *divine spark**). It has two aspects: *transcendent reason** and *executive reason*.*

Rotational movement: the imperceptible intrinsic movement which animates the individual from birth to death.

Saprophyte spirit: a spirit living in the surroundings of human beings that becomes pathogenic and attacks them when their *spiritual immune system** is weakened.

Self: the entity produced by the union of an *angelic soul** and a *basharic soul*.*

Self-regulated growth of the soul: the process of undergoing the different stages of the soul – childhood (immaturity), adolescence and maturity – under the direction of one's own judgment and will. This self-regulated growth cannot be achieved without the contribution of the body and the instructions of a divine being, and it begins at the moment when the body reaches the age of responsibility.

Sixth sense: a faculty of the *angelic soul** which allows one, among other things, to see God, to travel across time and space, to read the inner thoughts of people etc. Only God can awaken this sense.

Solvent of the soul: see *constituent substance of the soul*.

Spiritual allergy: an over-reaction of the spiritual immune system upon encountering a spiritual antigen to which it has already been exposed.

Spiritual amusements: parapsychological or even spiritual pleasures obtained through various techniques.

Spiritual antibody: a molecule made by one of the *spiritual micro-factories** of the *angelic soul*,* consisting of elements of the *worker self** and possessing the property of specifically combining with the *spiritual antigen** that triggered its fabrication in order to neutralize it.

Spiritual antigen: that which is recognized by the *angelic soul** as non-self, and which threatens to attack it, weaken it and make it ill or disrupt its growth.

Spiritual autoimmunity: a deviation of the spiritual immune system (due to the influence of spiritual microorganisms and toxins under favourable conditions) which causes the angelic soul to produce antibodies against one of its own constituents, having mistaken it for a foreign element.

Spiritual cell: see *spiritual zygote*.

Spiritual counterparts: spiritual creatures which, through their necessary union, generate a new and complete spiritual being apt for development (eg, the *angelic soul** and the *basharic soul**).

Spiritual ecosphere: the spiritual ecosystem comprising the spiritual environment (spiritual atmosphere, spiritual light) as well as all the spirits within it.

Spiritual immune system: all the mechanisms enabling the *angelic soul** to preserve its integrity against a great number of aggressors known as *spiritual antigens*.*

Spiritual lords: beings who have a spiritual rank equivalent to that of *archangels*.* They are the lords of every soul and, among other things, are in charge of divine missions and guidance.

Spiritual micro-factory: an immune cell of the *angelic soul** made of intentions and actions that are accomplished with the aim of divine satisfaction, and whose function is to produce antibodies for the soul.

Spiritual scientist: a divine person (prophet, saint) who possesses knowledge of the spiritual science.

Spiritual serotherapy: strengthening of the *spiritual immune system** through an injection into the *angelic soul** of a serum containing specific spiritual antibodies. Prayers, pilgrimages, a favourable spiritual environment, etc, can all play the role of such a serum.

Spiritual understanding: an understanding of the metaphysical dimension of human beings.

Spiritual vaccination: a strengthening of the spiritual immune system through the introduction into the *angelic soul** of *spiritual antigens** which have been rendered harmless.

Spiritual virus: a pathogenic spiritual agent that penetrates the *angelic soul** of an individual, altering the genetic code of its *transcendent reason** in such a way that the person loses the faculty of distinguishing right from wrong (he takes what is right to be wrong and what is wrong to be right) and in turn becomes pathogenic for others.

Spiritual zygote: a creature produced by the union of an *angelic soul** and a *basharic soul.**

Stomachic love: an attraction or weak point towards food and eating.

Tempter spirits (or diverting spirits): a *negative spirit** which has been created to tempt and test human beings who are on their way towards perfection.

Terrestrial gamete: see *basharic soul.*

Theophan: a *positive spirit** who is a manifestation of the divine essence.

Total concrete consciousness: the stage of consciousness in which one perceives the reality of the whole universe with such a degree of clarity that nothing remains unknown. It is the stage where the consciousness of a human being rejoins divine consciousness.

Total self: the self considered in both its dimensions, material and spiritual (physical and metaphysical).

Transcendent creativity: creativity whose origin transcends nature.

Transcendent intelligence (or conscious intelligence): an intelligence whose origin transcends nature and whose manifestations transcend natural instincts.

Transcendent reason: one of the aspects of *reason** (the other being *executive reason**). Transcendent reason is the eternal centre of *total concrete consciousness**: it is the centre of understanding the *real truth** of everything, of discerning between good and evil, usefulness and harm; it is the centre of free will, conscious or *transcendent will,** conscious intelligence, rational thought, *transcendent creativity,** *eternal memory** etc.

Transcendent will: a will whose origin transcends nature and whose manifestations consequently transcend natural instincts.

Translational movement: the movement which animates an individual from one life to the other, until he eventually reaches his own perfection.

True God: God as He is, and not as we imagine Him to be.

Vali: a partial or absolute *theophan** (absolute vali), representing God on Earth.

Vegetal spirit or soul: the vital essence which bestows life upon and animates the process of perfection of plants.

Venomous person: an individual who is highly toxic for the souls of those who are, spiritually speaking, still at the kindergarten or pre-school level; such a person can, through his words, actions or mere presence, divert others from authentic spirituality, all the more easily in that he often acts under the cover of religion or ethics and has a pleasant appearance which does not arouse suspicion.

Worker self: one of the two components of the *basharic soul** (the other being the *imperious self**); an instinctive and peaceful force which makes all the organs function together and ensures the preservation of life. For example, control of the automatic vegetative processes (eg, growth of the hair and nails) is one of its many functions.